Scotland

text and original photography by
Alex Ramsay

HarperCollins*Publishers*

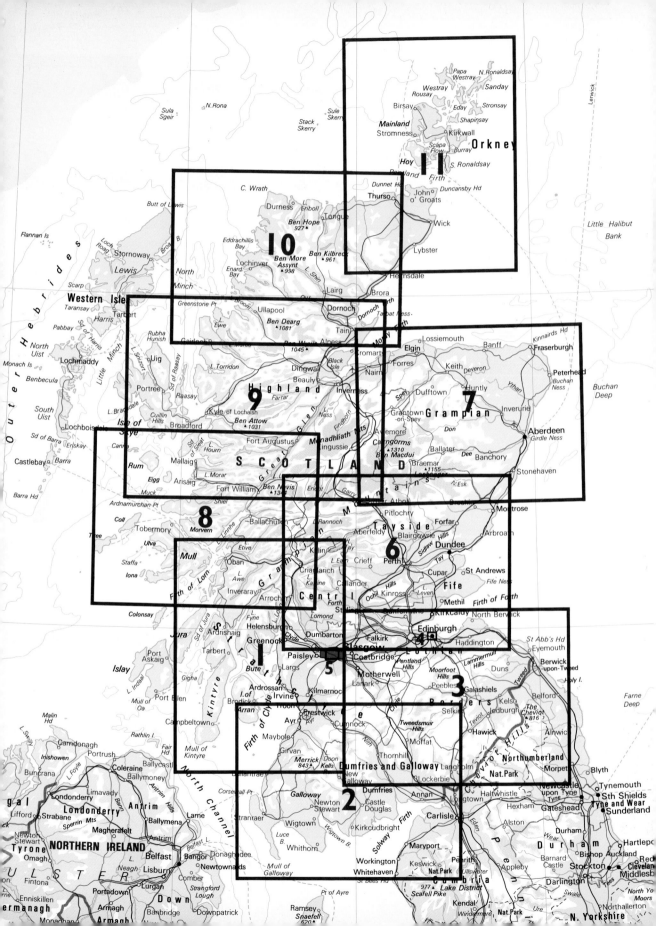

Contents

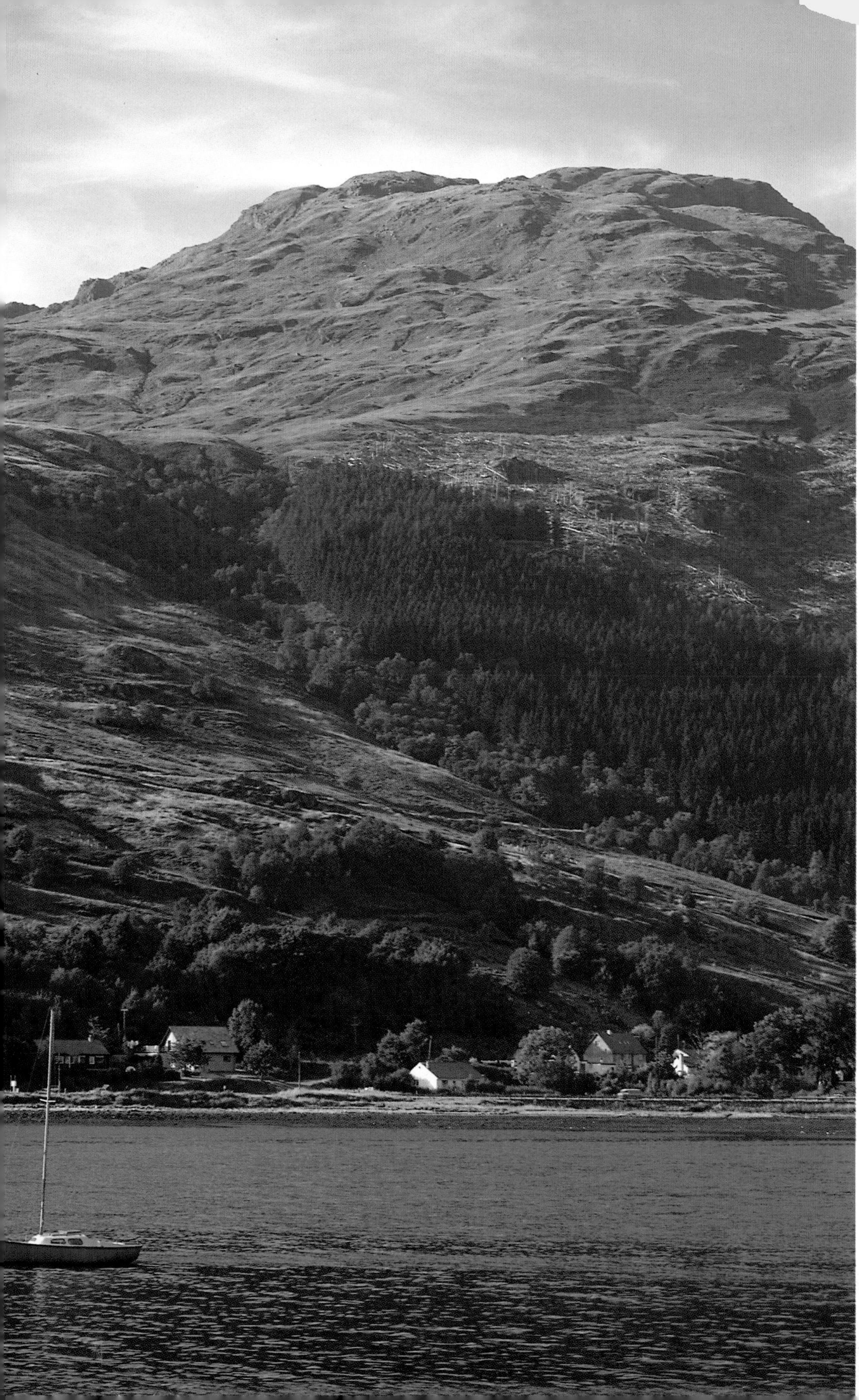

Strathclyde

Crinan Canal Basin (AA)

Glen Kinglas

Loch Lomond

Kilchurn Castle

Glasgow must surely be unique among the world's great industrial cities in having such glorious and wild countryside within easy reach. The city's surroundings are extra-ordinarily varied, from the busy holiday resorts of the Firth of Clyde to the remote yet beautiful islands of Colonsay and Oronsay.

Most of this area is Campbell country – the dominant branch of the clan lives at Inveraray, about 31 miles (49 km) north-west of Glasgow. However up until the end of the 15th century the area had been effectively ruled by the MacDonalds, who claimed the title of Lords of the Isles. The Campbells, who tended to side with the English ruling power (though not always), were often used by the English to put down Scottish rebellion among other clans. Although this increased their territory it also made them unpopular among the other Highland clans. Feuding was a way of life

Drawing-room, Hill House, Helensburgh (NTS)

among the clans, and life was frequently 'brutish, nasty and short'. The massacre of Glen Coe in 1692, in which Campbell troops quartered with the MacDonald clan at Glen Coe attacked their hosts, was the continuation of a centuries-old hatred between Campbell and MacDonald. Incidentally, you'll often see 'clan maps' on sale. These shouldn't be taken seriously – the whole idea of systematizing the clans is a very recent one and is based on very little historical information.

Colonsay, 25 miles (40 km) south of Mull, has the wonderfully mild Gulf Stream climate prevalent in this area. It is reputed that these West Coast islands receive more sunshine than anywhere else in Britain. Even when it does rain, it's rarely for long and when the sun returns it's so beautiful that you soon forget the drizzle. The water is unbelievably clear (a great deal cleaner than the Mediterranean, too) and there are shallow golden

View from Ben Lomond

Scottish Maritime Museum, Irvine (AA)

Cruachan power station

Dumbarton Castle (AA)

beaches everywhere. The famous white sand beaches are mostly farther north, where the coasts are open to the full force of the Atlantic. Colonsay itself is an island for exploring on foot. Look out for wild goats – they were once kept here for milk. At low tide you can get across to Oronsay – make sure you have read the tide-table correctly, or you'll be there until the next low tide. The remains of a 14th-century abbey can be found here. It was once a place of sanctuary. If a criminal could support himself for a year and a day on Oronsay,

he was allowed to go free. Incidentally, it's just possible to catch a glimpse of Ireland from here. St Columba did when he landed here in 563, and that's why he sailed farther on to Iona.

The island of Islay is famous for its distilleries, and also for the best cheese in Scotland. The whiskies owe their very distinctive flavours to the peaty waters of the island. It's quite possible to tell one distillery's product from another's, and it's certainly fun trying! Although the island produces its own single malts, most of the whisky goes to be

Castle Stalker (EPL)

blended – there's hardly a blended whisky in Scotland which doesn't contain some Islay malt. Don't miss the stunning Kildalton Cross in the south of the island. This was carved in the 9th century by a sculptor from Iona. It's often thought to be the finest in Scotland, and is beautifully situated. In the same area is the village of Bowmore, with a circular church – so that the devil couldn't find a corner to conceal himself in, or so the locals say.

There's plenty to see inland as well. A popular day out for many Glaswegians used to be a boat trip. Gourock was (and is) one of the main destinations for sailings from Glasgow. It's also a jumping-off point for the lovely Cowal peninsula. While you're in Gourock, have a look at Granny Kempoch's Stone, a prehistoric monolith thought by fishermen to bring fair winds as long as the appropriate rites were performed. From here there's a ferry service to Dunoon, saving a very long drive round the head of Loch Long. Dunoon is a popular place, very much a traditional resort.

Ben Tarsuin by Goatfell, Arran (NTS)

Inveraray Castle

At the end of August it has the Cowal Highland Gathering, where more than 150 pipe bands compete.

Nearby Holy Loch is said to derive its name from a shipwrecked boat that sailed from the Holy Land carrying consecrated soil to be placed in the foundations of Glasgow Cathedral. There's a pleasant little church on the shore of the loch at Kilmun. If you look in the graveyard you'll find some tombstones with the motto 'Free For a Blast' engraved on them. The motto is said to

refer to a hunt where the chieftain called off his dogs from their prey with a blast on his horn. This allowed the royal hounds to make the kill. The king was so grateful for this tactful gesture by his subject that he exempted the chieftain's family from paying taxes for ever.

The whole Cowal peninsula warrants exploration, and a visit to the magnificent Younger Botanic Garden is a must. This is one of the finest in an area famous for its gardens.

Alexandria, just south of Loch Lomond, has

Inveraray (AA)

Gourock, Firth of Clyde

Argyll Forest Park (AA)

something of interest for car enthusiasts. It was the home of the Argyll, Scotland's first home-produced car. The first one was built in 1899, and it was an immediate success. A magnificent neo-Baroque factory, still standing, was promptly built. Sadly, it proved just too magnificent. An Italian marble interior, 500 washbasins for the workforce and a resident Italian choir-master for the works choir put a heavy strain on the cash-flow, and the firm collapsed in 1908.

11

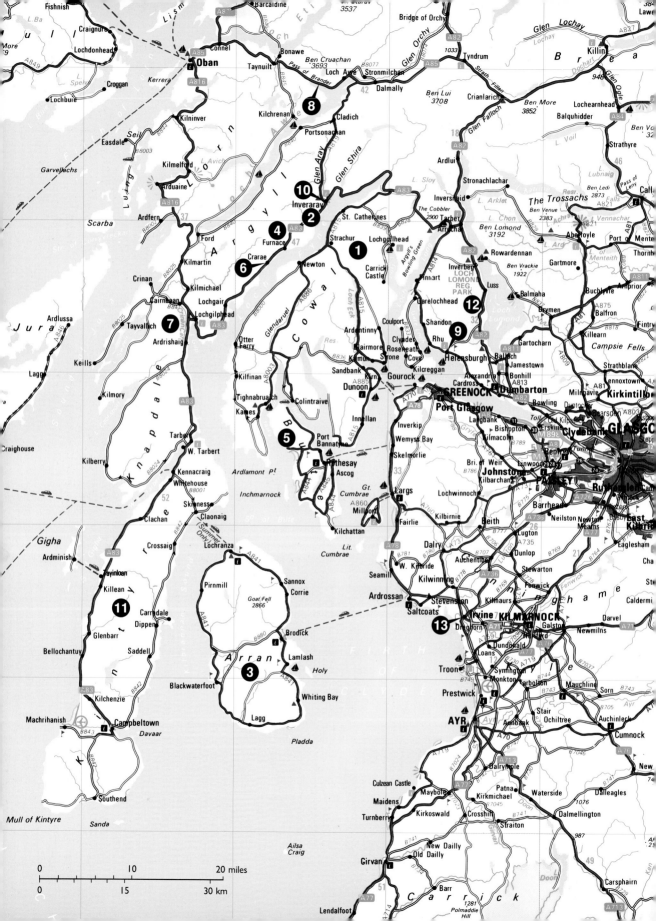

❶ ARGYLL FOREST PARK

This beautiful region has no fewer than 60,000 acres of forest and mountains rising to over 3000 feet (915 m). It was the first Forestry Commission forestry park to be created in Britain (in 1935). There are plenty of marked trails and the highest point is called Rest and be Thankful, from an inscription on a stone erected by the men who made the road in 1750. It's easy to understand their feelings!

❷ ARGYLL WILDLIFE PARK

Overlooking Loch Fyne, the park has a great variety of Scottish wildlife, including many rare and protected creatures such as badgers, Highland foxes and wildcats. There are many foreign species not common to Scotland as well, and a number of rare owls.

❸ ARRAN

Arran, like Bute, is a popular holiday island. However, even at the height of the season you can escape the crowds. Heading up to Goat Fell, the highest point (2841 ft/874 m), is an attractive walk with terrific views from the summit. With luck you may see golden eagles circling over the hills from here. Brodick is the island's capital with all the resources you'd expect of a holiday centre. Brodick Castle was once Robert the Bruce's headquarters. It now houses good collections of paintings, silver and porcelain and other antiquities. Refreshments available. (Open Easter–Sept daily ₺ ₰. Phone 01770 302202) The castle gardens are also splendid, particularly in the spring.

❹ AUCHINDRAIN

This is one of the few West Highland villages to survive almost completely unchanged. The original 18th- and 19th-century longhouses and barns are still standing and most have their original furnishings and equipment. At certain times you can watch demonstrations of weaving and other crafts.

❺ BUTE

Bute, and especially its main town Rothesay, has for generations been one of Glasgow's main holiday resorts. There's plenty to do, especially for the young – but unless you like crowds avoid the peak season. The 13th-century moated castle in the middle of the town is magnificent. Its circular plan is unique in this part of the country. ☎ 01700 502151

❻ CRARAE GARDEN

A splendid woodland garden set in a Highland glen. The rhododendrons and azaleas are glorious in early summer, and autumn is equally spectacular. (Open all year daily. Phone 01546 86614)

❼ CRINAN CANAL

The 18th-century canal, with its 15 locks, runs from Loch Fyne to the Sound of Jura, a distance of 9 miles (14 km). Before it was built boats had to sail 130 miles (208 km) round the hazardous Kintyre peninsula.

❽ CRUACHAN POWER STATION

The vast hydro-electric station is hidden inside Ben Cruachan above Loch Awe. The only trace of it is the dam, 1300 feet (390 m) up the mountain. It's a staggering achievement and well worth a visit – a bus takes you along a tunnel deep into the heart of the mountain. (Open Apr–Oct daily. Phone 01866 62673) Don't miss the dramatic view of Kilchurn Castle at the head of the loch. This Campbell stronghold was built in 1440.

❾ THE HILL HOUSE

Designed in 1902 by Charles Rennie Mackintosh, The Hill House at Helensburgh gives you a chance to see how he brought architecture and interior decoration into harmony. The extraordinary chairs make a lot more sense when you see them in the house for which they were designed. Refreshments available. (Open Apr–Dec daily, afternoons) The town, laid out in 1776, is itself a popular resort. ☎ 01436 672642

❿ INVERARAY

This small town owes its existence to the rebuilding of Inveraray Castle. The region is largely owned by the Campbells, Dukes of Argyll since 1701. Having been handsomely rewarded for their loyalty to King George II during the Jacobite rebellion of 1745, they decided to replace their 15th-century home with the present neo-Gothic castle. (Open early Apr–mid Oct, Sat–Thurs; July–Aug, daily ₰. Phone 01499 2203) The castle was finished in 1770. The interior is very impressive, with a wonderful collection of treasures, including 1300 pieces of weaponry. In the grounds is the Combined Operations Museum. Explore Inveraray Jail, an award-winning 'living' 19th-century prison (some of the exhibits are fairly gruesome). (Open all year daily. Phone 01499 2381)

⓫ KINTYRE

This long peninsula is all but an island. In fact in the 11th century Magnus Barefoot, having been granted any land he could take his ship around 'with rudder in place', dragged his ships across the narrow strip of land at Tarbert and claimed Kintyre. The famous Mull of Kintyre is the southernmost point (only 13 miles/20 km from Ireland). Campbeltown is the holiday centre for Kintyre – Machrihanish Bay a few miles away has good beaches. There's also a golf course.

⓬ LOCH LOMOND

This famous loch deserves its reputation as one of the most beautiful. It's well worth taking the road along the east side, as far as it goes. The views are just as good, and it's much more peaceful than the A82. You can take cruises on the loch from Balloch, Tarbet, Luss and Balmaha. From Rowardennan you can climb Ben Lomond.

⓭ SCOTTISH MARITIME MUSEUM, IRVINE

A lively, active museum project which tells the story of Scotland's maritime history. There's plenty to see (both indoors and out), from a shipyard worker's tenement flat to a huge collection of vessels of all types and sizes, including a clipper and a Clyde 'puffer'. (Open Apr–Oct, daily ₰. Phone 01294 278283) **13**

The South-West

Preceding page: Durrisdeer

Orangery, Culzean Country Park (NTS)

Threave Castle, Stranraer

Gatehouse, Culzean Castle

Castle Kennedy Gardens (D&G TB)

The south-west corner of Scotland is definitely the place to come for real tranquillity. It's probably the least-known part of the country, yet offers everything from wild scenery to lively coastal resorts and historic towns with centuries-old traditions.

Ayr, and the countryside around it, is of course world-famous as the place where Robert Burns spent his early years. Those familiar with the works of Scotland's greatest dialect poet will recognize every name round here. The landscape has hardly changed since Burns wrote about it in the 18th century.

Burns is by no means the only literary link this area possesses. Addicts of Dorothy L. Sayers can try following the complicated wanderings of Lord Peter Wimsey and the suspected murderers in *Five Red Herrings*; these take place in the area around Kirkcudbright. Another detective hero, John Buchan's Richard Hannay, was pursued through the countryside around Newton Stewart (in *The Thirty-Nine Steps*). If you're interested, a lot of the

Sweetheart Abbey, New Abbey

Threave Castle ferry

New Abbey

Farm, Galloway

action is set in Bargaly Glen, a few miles southeast of the town.

The whole area is rich in traditional celebrations. Many Border towns have their 'Common Ridings' or 'Riding of the Marches'. These processions on horseback recall the days when the men would have to defend the town against cattle raiders (often English). There's often a fair and other events; the 'Guid Nychburris' celebrations in Dumfries last a whole week! These festivities take place throughout the summer so there's bound to

17

Caerlaverock Castle

Cairnholy I neolithic cairn

Girvan

Lowther Hills above Durisdeer

Girvan beach

Dulveen Pass

Grey Mare's Tail

be one coinciding with your holiday. For something different try Palnackie, where they have the World Flounder Tramping Championship. This involves wiggling your bare toes in the mud until you find your flounder — yes, it's perfectly true. There's another odd thing about this pretty little port; it's said there used to be a Palnackie Treacle Works (sugar was once imported through here) where the workers trod out the treacle. Their wages, so they say, were a halfpenny a week and their feet to lick . . . One custom that has died out was the annual Handfasting Fair in Eskdalemuir. Unmarried boys and girls were paired off for a year's trial 'marriage'. At the next fair the 'handfast' was reconsidered. If it hadn't worked out the couple would separate, and any resulting children would go with the unsatisfied partner. This continued well into the 18th century. Eskdalemuir, incidentally, is the site of Europe's largest Buddhist monastery.

In many places throughout the south-west you'll come across monuments erected in memory of the Covenanters. This movement began in the 1630s when King Charles I tried to impose English forms of worship upon the Church of Scotland. Riots broke out, and thousands of Scots signed the 'Covenant' binding them to resist any attempt by the Crown to interfere in Scottish religious matters. A series of battles between Covenanters and Royalists followed (the 'Bishop's Wars'). By the 1660s many people had chosen to worship in freedom in the hills. These meetings (conventicles) were declared treasonable in 1670, and years of persecution followed (the 'killing time'). The last Covenanter was executed in 1688. It was a cruel period, the memory of which lives on. In Wigtown you can see where Margaret McLauchlan and Margaret Wilson were tied to stakes on the shore and left to the rising tide. In Douglas a stone commemorates the covenanting tailor whose ears were cut off with his own shears. On his return from exile he carved his own memorial to this brutal act.

The west coast is very different from the quiet Solway Firth. The remote Mull of Galloway forms the southernmost tip of Scotland (a tribe of cannibals lived here well into medieval times). Farther up the coast the resort towns begin. The main one is Girvan, with a busy harbour and lots for the children to do. The horizon is dominated by Ailsa Craig, known as 'Paddy's Milestone' — it's halfway between Glasgow and Belfast.

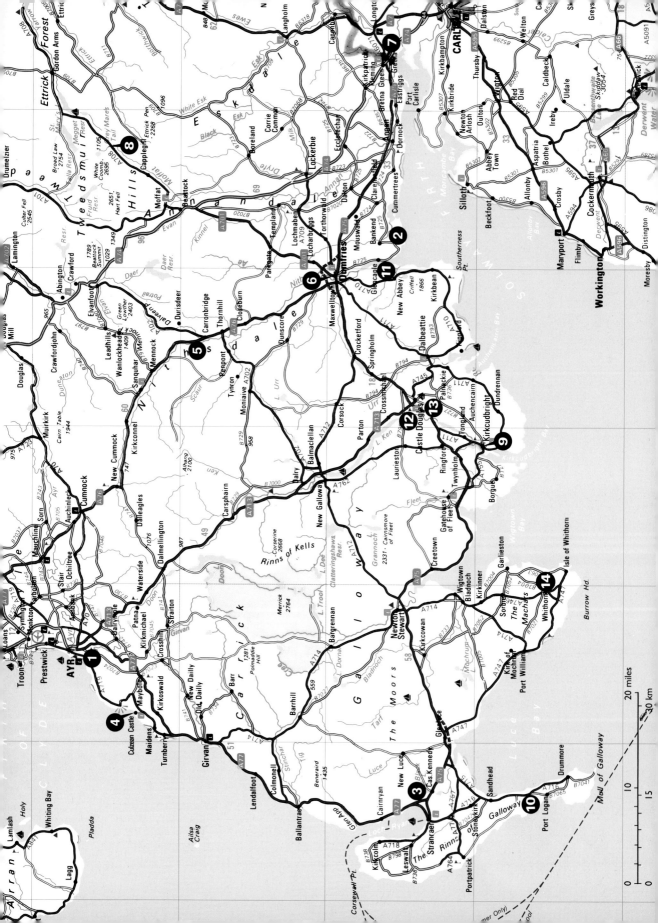

1 ALLOWAY

Situated on the edge of Ayr, the village was the birthplace of Robert Burns, born in 1759. The cottage that his father built still stands. (Open Apr–Oct daily; Nov–Mar, Sun afternoons only. Phone 01292 441215) The Land o' Burns Visitor Centre (open daily, all year. Phone 01292 443700) has a multimedia presentation of Burns's favourite poem *Tam o' Shanter*, and you can see the landmarks featured in the poem, the Auld Kirk and the Brig o' Doon, in the village itself.

2 CAERLAVEROCK CASTLE

This late 13th-century castle is everything a ruined castle should be, with its tall towers reflected in the waters of the moat. It's built in the form of a triangle with a tower at each point. Inside is what remains of a once famous and wonderfully graceful Renaissance-style interior (1634), known as 'Lord Nithsdale's Daintie Fabrick'. (Open all year, Mon–Sat and Sun afternoon. Phone 01387 777275)

3 CASTLE KENNEDY GARDENS

Wonderful grounds originally inspired by Versailles, and set around the Black and White lochs. There are romantic castle ruins, a lily pond, monkey puzzle trees and a wonderful springtime display of rhododendrons and azaleas. Refreshments available. (Open Apr–Sept daily ♿. Phone 01776 702024)

4 CULZEAN CASTLE AND COUNTRY PARK

Splendidly situated on a clifftop overlooking the Firth of Clyde, the castle was built by Robert Adam between 1772 and 1792. Refreshments available. (Open Apr–Oct daily ♿ 🐴. Phone 01655 760269) There are beautiful 18th-century gardens and 560 acres of parkland, with an adventure playground, woodland walks and a deer park. (Open all year daily 🐴)

5 DRUMLANRIG CASTLE AND COUNTRY PARK

This is the home of the Duke of Buccleuch and Queensberry and dates back to the 1680s. It is notable for its fine art collection, plasterwork and carving. There's an adventure playground, a craft centre and tea rooms. You can also hire bicycles to explore the beautiful parklands. (Castle open May–Aug, Fri–Wed 🐴. Phone 01848 330248. Park open daily)

6 DUMFRIES

A handsome town on the River Nith, where Robert Burns spent his last years. His house with its collection of relics is open to the public. (Phone 01387 64808) There's also a Burns Centre with an exhibition and audio-visual displays. The museum has a Camera Obscura – this was the equivalent of going to the cinema 150 years ago! (Phone 01387 53374) (All open Apr–Sept, Mon–Sat and Sun afternoon; Oct–Mar Camera Obscura closed; museum closed Mon.)

7 GRETNA GREEN

This little village standing right on the border with England is world-famous for its romantic associations. It was in the smithy here that thousands of couples were married under Scots law, which required no banns or licences, throughout the last century. All that was needed was a declaration in front of witnesses, so runaway lovers from all over England used to come here, often with angry relatives hot on their trail. ℹ 01461 337834

8 GREY MARE'S TAIL

There are several other waterfalls in Scotland with the same name, but at 200 feet (60 m) this is the highest. It's by the main road between Moffat and St Mary's Loch. You can walk up to the top, but it's dangerous when wet and care should be taken with children.

9 KIRKCUDBRIGHT

Pronounced 'Kircoobrie', this pretty 18th-century town is a centre for artists from all over Scotland. There are exhibitions throughout the summer. At the harbour don't miss McLellan's Castle, built in 1582. (Open all year, Mon–Sat and Sun afternoon) If you'd like to know more about local history there's an exhibition in the Stewartry Museum. (Open Mar–Oct, Mon–Sat; Jun–Sep, Sun afternoons; Nov–Feb, Sat only. Phone 01557 331643) ℹ 01557 330494

10 LOGAN BOTANIC GARDENS

Subtropical gardens, with cabbage palms and spectacular tree ferns. Nearby is the 18th-century tidal fishpond, where the fish can be fed by hand. (Open Mar–Oct daily. Phone 01776 860231)

11 SWEETHEART ABBEY

The abbey takes its name from the fact that its founder, Devorguilla Balliol, carried her husband's embalmed heart with her after his death. Devorguilla (founder of Balliol College, Oxford) was eventually buried together with the heart in front of the altar. (Open all year daily; closed Thu afternoon and Fri, Oct–Mar) Nearby Shambellie House has a costume museum. (Open Apr–Oct daily. Phone 01387 850375)

12 THREAVE CASTLE

One of the best things about this fine 14th-century castle is the way you approach it. Park your car beside a farmyard and follow a footpath across the fields until you reach the River Dee. Ring the bell that hangs there, and wait until the ferryman arrives to take you across to the island on which the castle stands. It was built by Archibald the Grim, 3rd Earl of Douglas, but was wrecked when the Covenanters took it in 1640. (Open Apr–Sept, Mon–Sat and Sun afternoon)

13 THREAVE GARDEN

All year this extensive garden has a great variety of interesting plants, but the best time to visit is spring, when over 200 varieties of daffodil provide a stunning spectacle. Refreshments available. (Open all year daily ♿. Phone 01556 502575)

14 WHITHORN DIG VISITOR CENTRE

The site of Scotland's first Christian settlement. Whithorn, Cradle of Christianity, gives entry to the Priory Museum, the Whithorn Dig and Discovery Centre. (Open Apr–Oct, daily. Phone 01988 500508)

Borders and Lothian

Borders farm

Floors Castle, Kelso

House of the Binns, Linlithgow (AA)

Linlithgow Palace

St Abbs (AA)

Forth Rail Bridge

The wild and empty moorland of the Border Region is probably the most fought-over country in Britain. From the days of the Romans until the 18th century there was hardly a break in the sequence of raid and counter-raid across the border, interspersed with the occasional full-scale war. As a result you'll see ruined castles and pele towers everywhere.

Those warlike days are commemorated in many Border towns by the annual 'Common Ridings'. These spectacular events usually involve riding around the town boundaries on horseback, often accompanied by traditional celebrations. They take place throughout the summer months.

The Borders proper are the most southerly part of Scotland. Moving north, you come to the Lammermuir Hills. Beautiful at any time, they're at their best in August when the heather is in flower. Everywhere you go the air will be filled with the rich honey-smell of heather. Don't fail to buy some local honey – there are beehives all over the hillsides in summer. Farther north still you'll see the massive hump of the Bass Rock emerging from the sea. This gigantic mound of basalt is the far end of a chain of such hills that stretches right across Scotland. Both Edinburgh Castle and Stirling Castle are built on them. It was the only rock hard enough to withstand the enormous pressure of the glaciers of the Ice Age. All but inaccessible, the Bass Rock has been a hermitage, a prison and a fortress at different times. There's a good view of it to be had from Berwick Law, another in the chain. Witches were once burned up here. There's also an arch made of a whale's jawbones. You may see others along the east

Stairway and cupola, Hopetoun House (SCOTTISH TB)

Bass Rock from Berwick Law

Neidpath Castle, Peebles

coast, indicators of links with the whaling trade in days gone by.

The name most closely linked with this countryside is that of Sir Walter Scott, the famous poet, novelist and antiquarian. He was devoted to his country, and his knowledge of it was enormous. The historical novels in particular are as precise as years of research and thousands of miles of travelling could make them. What many people don't know is that it was Scott who revived, almost singlehandedly, the Scottish traditions of dress and music. These had all but disappeared after the battle of Culloden in 1746, when everything distinctly Highland – the tartan and the pipes – was made illegal. His first triumph was the rediscovery of the Scottish Regalia – the Crown, Sceptre and other items. These had been lost since 1707. Scott discovered them personally in Edinburgh Castle in 1817. He then organized the first visit to Scotland by a reigning monarch for 150 years. When George IV arrived in Holyrood the palace was filled with the banned trappings of the Highlands. Even the king dressed with enthusiasm in the Royal Stuart tartan. Don't miss Scott's View

Traquair House, Innerleithen

Scott's View, near Dryburgh

Preston Mill, near Dunbar

(signposted from Dryburgh) over the triple peaks of the Eildon Hills. It's best seen in the morning. Scott was so fond of this view that the horses pulling his funeral cortege stopped here of their own accord.

The principal industry of the Borders is of course textiles, and its most famous product is tweed. Oddly enough this has nothing to do with the river, but comes from a clerk's misreading of the technical word 'tweel' when the first batches arrived in London. Originally the only colours were blue, black or grey. Then the weavers of Jedburgh started twisting different coloured strands together to make the patterns that everyone knows today. Natural sources were used for dyes – green came from broom, yellow from rhubarb, among others. The dyers probably had the worst job in the mill – the colours were fixed with urine, which they had to collect each morning from the neighbouring houses. At least one phrase from the industry has entered the language; to ensure that the cloth dries evenly it's put into a tentering machine and stretched until taut – on tenterhooks.

❶ ABBOTSFORD HOUSE

This was the home of Sir Walter Scott for the last 20 years of his life. His descendants still live here. It's a fascinating house, built to Scott's own Romantic design, and crammed with his collection of curios, many of which have Scottish connections. Refreshments. (Open mid Mar–Oct, Mon–Sat daily and Sun afternoon ♿. Phone 01896 2043)

❷–❺ THE BORDER ABBEYS

These four beautiful buildings all stand within 12 miles of each other. Melrose (2) was founded by David I in 1136 and restored in the 19th century by Sir Walter Scott. Look out for the rooftop carving of a pig playing the bagpipes! The ruined abbey of Jedburgh (3) still dominates the skyline, while Dryburgh (4) is the burial place of Sir Walter Scott and Field Marshal Haig. The partial remains of Kelso Abbey (5) still bear testimony to fine 12th-century craftsmanship. (All open all year, Mon–Sat and Sun afternoon)

❻ THE FORTH BRIDGES

The Forth Rail Bridge is one of the most famous bridges in the world, and one of the greatest feats of engineering ever performed. It was built between 1883 and 1890. It's well over a mile long and 361 feet (108 m) high, with a clearance for shipping of 150 feet (45 m). It's painted continuously, taking three years to cover the 135 acres of steel. The Road Bridge, finished in 1964, is completely different in style but nonetheless a graceful structure. It has a central span of 3300 feet (990 m) and the suspension towers are 512 feet (153 m) high. A good way to see the Rail Bridge is to take the ferry to Inchcolm Island, where there are the remains of the 12th-century St Columba's Abbey.

❼ HERMITAGE CASTLE

This huge and lonely fortress has a peculiarly sinister atmosphere. In 1342 Sir Alexander Ramsay was starved to death here by the Douglases. He managed to survive for 3 weeks on the grains of corn that dropped from the granary above the dungeon. Mary Queen of Scots paid a visit to the castle in 1566. (Open Apr–Sept, Mon–Sat and Sun afternoon; Oct–Mar, Sat and Sun afternoon only. Phone 0131 244 3101)

❽ HOPETOUN HOUSE

One of the very finest 18th-century houses in Scotland. It was begun in 1699 and continued throughout the 18th century by the Adam family, father and sons. It's furnished with great magnificence as it was in 1760. You'll find paintings by Rubens, Canaletto and Titian among others. There are exhibitions, deer parks, nature trails and a restaurant. (Open Apr–Sept daily. Phone 0131 331 2451)

❾ HOUSE OF THE BINNS

This beautiful 17th-century house is the home of the Dalyell family. It was the first house given to the National Trust for Scotland, in 1944. Apart from the finely moulded plaster ceilings, the house is interesting for its relics of the 17th-century General Tam Dalyell. He led a dramatic life including an escape from the Tower of London and service under the Russian Tsar. In 1666 he defeated the Covenanters as they marched on Edinburgh. (House open May–Sept daily, except Friday, afternoons only. Phone 01506 834255 to check opening times during restoration work. Parkland, open daily ♿)

❿ LINLITHGOW PALACE

The birthplace of Mary Queen of Scots, the palace was built mainly during the 15th and 16th centuries. Though it's now beside the loch, it was probably once completely surrounded by water. The splendid fountain was given by James V (Mary's father) as a wedding present to his wife, Mary of Guise. It is said to have run with wine on many great royal occasions. Open all year, Mon–Sat and Sun afternoon. Phone 0131 2443101)

⓫ PRESTON MILL

Restored by the National Trust for Scotland, this is the last working watermill on the River Tyne. Built in the 16th century, it's a quaint little building with a tall conical roof and wind vane. This is known locally as the 'long arm of friendship'. It's a very picturesque spot, with a flock of geese on the millpond. (Open Apr–Sept, Mon–Sat and Sun afternoon; Oct weekends only ♿. Phone 01620 860426)

⓬ TANTALLON CASTLE

The spectacular position with cliffs on three sides and a moat around the fourth must have been a daunting prospect for any attacking force. Built in 1375, this Douglas stronghold stood intact until the Cromwellian General Monk brought his cannon against it in 1651. Don't miss the view from the battlements of the Bass Rock out to sea. (Open Apr–Sept, Mon–Sat and Sun afternoon; Oct–Mar, Mon–Wed and Sat; Thurs and Sun afternoons. Phone 0131 244 3101)

⓭ THIRLESTANE CASTLE

One of Scotland's oldest and finest castles. Inside there are magnificent ceilings, and toy and country life exhibitions. Children can dress up and play with the toys in the nursery. (Open Easter, May–Sep, Mon, Wed, Thurs, Sun; plus July–Aug, Tue and Fri. Afternoons only ♿. Phone 01578 722430)

⓮ TRAQUAIR HOUSE

This splendid building has been continuously inhabited for more than 1000 years. The Stuarts of Traquair were passionate supporters of the Stuart Kings, and the great Bear Gates of the estate have remained closed ever since Bonnie Prince Charlie passed through them in 1745. Closed they will stay until there's a Stuart on the throne again. Traquair is unique in another respect – it has its own 18th-century brewhouse, producing a fine ale. There are tastings every Friday afternoon during the summer. There are a number of craft workshops in the grounds, and even a maze to lose the children in! Refreshments are available. (Open Easter, May, June and Sept daily from 1230; July and Aug daily from 1030; Oct, Fri–Sun from 1400. Phone 01896 830323)

Edinburgh

Preceding page: **Heriot's Hospital** (foreground)

Grassmarket

Calton Hill

Royal Museum of Scotland (AA)

W ithout any question this is one of the world's great cities. Its dramatic beauty, its architectural diversity and its place at the centre of Scotland's history combine to make it an essential place to visit. The quality of its cultural and intellectual life has been world-famous for at least four centuries.

When describing Edinburgh you have to begin with the Castle. Perched on its great rock like a bird of prey it dominates almost every view of the city. Such a strong position is likely to have been

fortified since the arrival of the first men, though there's little if any evidence for this. The position was even stronger than it appears today, as there was a loch (the Nor'loch) around the base of the rock as well as an impassable marsh. The city is thought to take its name from a 6th-century fortification called Dun Eadain, the 'fortress on the slope'.

It's easiest to think of Edinburgh as divided into two, the Old Town and the New Town. The Old Town arose as a line of houses running down the

North Bridge (AA)

Princes Street from Ramsay Gardens

spine of rock from the Castle along what is now the Royal Mile. It effectively filled the area between the Royal Mile and Cowgate, and is endlessly fascinating to explore. The Old Town was cramped inside the city walls so that the only way to expand was upwards. This means that many of the 16th- and 17th-century buildings are of exceptional height, divided by the narrow little alleys called 'wynds'. A winding common staircase usually gives access to all floors. You'll find that the stairs in the older buildings always wind clockwise so that the defender would have more room for sword-play than his opponent. There was no drainage in those days, of course, so everything (chamber-pots included) was simply tipped out of the windows. There would be a warning cry of 'Gardy-loo' (*Gare de l'eau*) followed by a deluge – you'd be lucky if it was just 'eau'! One of the interesting side-effects of this communal way of living is sometimes thought to be the relatively class-free atmosphere of Edinburgh. In the same house it would be common

33

Salisbury Crags and Arthur's Seat (EPL)

The Mound from Ramsay Lane

Charlotte Square

to find a lord in the grand first-floor rooms, a lawyer above him, then perhaps a seamstress, a student, and so on. They would all have shared the same door and been aware (to a greater extent than in England) of 'how the other half lived'.

Don't miss the areas of the Grassmarket and Greyfriars, at the foot of the Castle Rock. The first was for many years the place where Covenanters were executed. Around the corner, Greyfriars Churchyard was the scene of the signing of the National Covenant in 1638. The soot-blackened tombstones are fascinatingly elaborate. You'll notice that (here and elsewhere in Scotland) some of them are enclosed in heavy iron cages. These are called mort-safes, and were intended to thwart the activities of the body-snatchers. Edinburgh was (and is) a great centre for medical research, and

Making kilts in the Royal Mile (AA)

bodies for dissection fetched a high price. The men who stole them were known, with grisly humour, as 'resurrection-men'. The trade fell into even greater disrepute when two of them, the notorious Burke and Hare, decided to save themselves the effort of digging up the coffins. They murdered 18 people and sold their bodies before being caught in 1828. Their business was run from a house just off the nearby West Port. Also in the churchyard you'll find the grave of John Gray. After his death in 1848 his terrier Bobby watched over his grave for 14 years. There's a statue of Bobby in Candlemaker Row close by, with a plaque recording his loyalty.

All this is a far cry from the grace and style of the New Town. This northern half of the city was designed about 1770, and it remains the finest Georgian urban landscape in the world. It's 35

Edinburgh Castle

Cat napping

The Mound and National Gallery

Frederick Street

Greyfriar's Churchyard

reached by crossing the Mound, built from the excavated soil of the new buildings. Princes Street Gardens on either side were at that time under the waters of the Nor'loch, which wasn't drained until 1816. The city was thus divided in half. Anyone who could afford to move from the stinking warrens of the Old Town did so, and it began its slide into the slum condition from which it has only recently recovered.

Walking anywhere in the New Town will give you its flavour, but the one unmissable sight is Charlotte Square, designed by Robert Adam. The town's light and airy feel is helped by the occasional glimpses of the Firth of Forth. Beyond the New Town is Telford's Dean Bridge, built in 1832 100 feet (30 m) above the Water of Leith. Cross the bridge and you reach Dean Village, a 16th-century quarter in the heart of Edinburgh where the millers worked. It's worth making your way out to Leith (you can do it on foot if you want, as there's a path following the course of the river). This was Edinburgh's old port. It was at

Crown of St Giles and Tron Church

Bank Street

Scott Monument (AA)

Leith that Mary Queen of Scots landed on her return to Edinburgh in 1561. The house where she was received, Andrew Lamb's house, is still standing.

If you're thinking of staying in Edinburgh during the last three weeks of August, forget it (unless you've booked well in advance). This is Festival time, when the city's population literally doubles overnight. The main International Festival brings the world's greatest companies and performers to Edinburgh. There's also the Festival Fringe, with at least 500 performances daily lasting far into the night. Old Festival hands compete to see the greatest number of productions in a day. All the performance space in the city is taken up – some people really have staged shows in telephone kiosks. The streets are filled with entertainers – in fact it's something that must be experienced. The Military Tattoo at the Castle is world-famous, and the Glenlivet Fireworks Concert, a spectacular display set to music, is normally held on the last Thursday of the Festival or Tattoo.

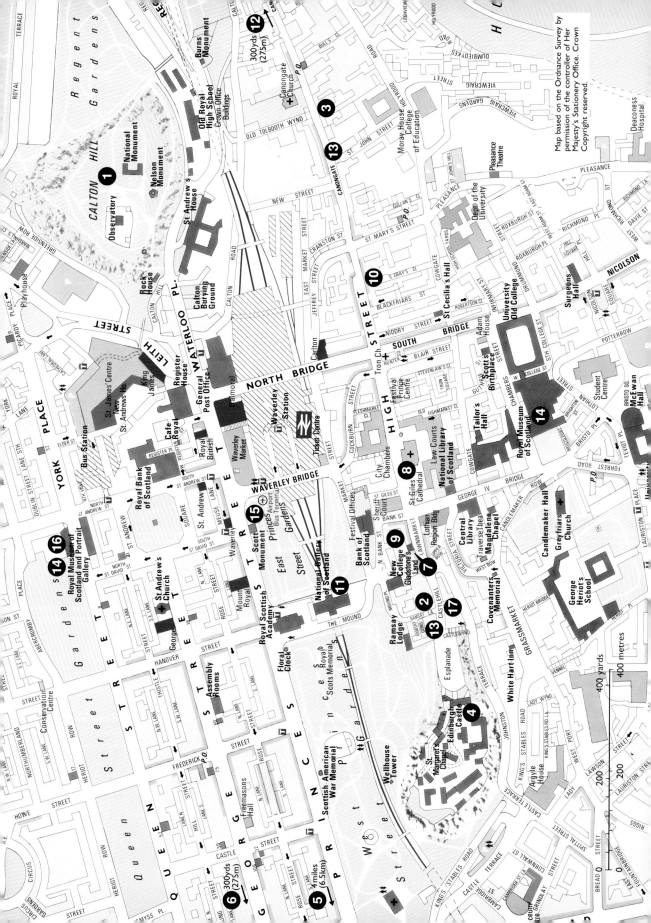

❶ CALTON HILL

There are some of the best views of the city from here. It's covered in rather eccentric monuments. There's one to Lord Nelson shaped like a telescope, and the unfinished 'Parthenon', in fact the 'National Monument'. This was started in memory of the casualties of the Napoleonic Wars, but the funds raised for it ran out.

❷ CAMERA OBSCURA

Situated in the Outlook Tower just off the Lawnmarket, this 19th-century predecessor to the cinema projects a panoramic view of the whole city onto a horizontal screen by slowly rotating a series of mirrors on top of the tower. (Open daily. Phone 0131 226 3709)

❸ CANONGATE TOLBOOTH AND HUNTLY HOUSE MUSEUM

Once the meeting place of the town council, the handsome 16th-century Tolbooth now houses The People's Story, focusing on the lives of ordinary Edinburgh folk, from the 18th century on. Displays include the reconstruction of a cooper's workshop and a 1940s kitchen. Opposite is Huntly House (1570), with exhibits of Scottish pottery and Edinburgh silver and glass. (Both Canongate. Open all year, Mon–Sat; Sun afternoon during Festival. Phone 0131 225 2424)

❹ EDINBURGH CASTLE

This splendid fortress dominates the city skyline. The first building on the site was 12th-century St Margaret's Chapel, the oldest building in Edinburgh. Here is Mons Meg cannon, used in the siege of Threave Castle in 1455. The cannon was brought back to Edinburgh by Sir Walter Scott in 1829. Don't miss the Crown Room containing the Scottish Regalia (rediscovered by Scott in 1817) and the royal apartments. The esplanade is the site of the famous Military Tattoo. (Open Mon–Sat, and Sun afternoon. Phone 0131 244 3101) Near here, from the Half-Moon Battery, a gun is fired daily at one o'clock, as it has since 1861.

❺ EDINBURGH ZOO

Founded in 1913, the zoo has the largest collection of animals in Scotland. Children will enjoy the famous Penguin Parade. (Corstorphine Road. Open daily. Phone 0131 334 9171)

❻ GEORGIAN HOUSE

Number 7 Charlotte Square shows the civilized pleasures of living in the New Town in the 18th century. Designed by Robert Adam, it has been restored and furnished in the contemporary style. (Open Apr–Oct, Mon–Sat and Sun afternoon. Phone 0131 225 2160)

❼ GLADSTONE'S LAND

A six-storey merchant's house dated 1620. It has several fine painted ceilings; worth visiting for the picture it gives of life in the Old Town. (447B Lawnmarket. Open Apr–Oct daily and Sun afternoon. Phone 0131 226 5856)

❽ HIGH KIRK OF ST GILES

The amazing structure that caps the tower of this 15th-century church is known as the 'Crown of St Giles' – there are only two others like it in the country. (Open Mon–Sat and Sun afternoon. Phone 0131 225 4363)

❾ THE WRITERS' MUSEUM

A fine early 17th-century house with a large collection of memorabilia belonging to Scott, Burns and Stevenson. (Lawnmarket. Open Mon–Sat and Sun afternoons in Aug. Phone 0131 225 2424)

❿ MUSEUM OF CHILDHOOD

Home of a unique collection of historic children's items and displays. (42 High Street. Open all year Mon–Sat, and Sun afternoon in Aug. Phone 0131 225 2424)

⓫ NATIONAL GALLERY OF SCOTLAND

This stands next to the Royal Scottish Academy. Between them they contain a really outstanding collection of pictures – contemporary Scottish work being found in the Academy. (The Mound. Open Mon–Sat and Sun afternoon ♿. Phone 0131 556 8921)

⓬ PALACE OF HOLYROODHOUSE

This is the Queen's official home when in Edinburgh. It was built about 1500 by James IV. Its romantic fame stems from its links with Mary Queen of Scots, and the 'Historical Apartments' where she lived are most interesting. You can see the room where Mary was dining with her secretary Rizzio before her husband Lord Darnley burst in and dragged him away to his death. (Open daily, except during royal visits. Phone 0131 556 1096) You can also walk into Holyrood Park, which leads to the volcanic outcrop of Arthur's Seat.

⓭ ROYAL MILE

This is the name given to the road that runs from the castle down to Holyrood. From the top, it consists of Castle Hill, the Lawnmarket, the High Street and Canongate.

⓮ MUSEUM OF ANTIQUITIES

An impressive building holding outstanding collections on archaeology, natural history, geology, science and many others. Refreshments. (Queen St. and Chambers St. Open Mon–Sat and Sun afternoon ♿. Phone 0131 225 7534)

⓯ SCOTT MONUMENT

You can climb this 200 foot (60 m) spire for a good view of the Old Town. It was put up in 1846 and is decorated with figures from Scott's novels. (East Princes St. Gardens. Open Mon–Sat, also Sun, June–Sept. Phone 0131 225 2424)

⓰ SCOTTISH NATIONAL PORTRAIT GALLERY

This outstanding collection covers most of the Scots who have made a mark on Scottish history. (Queen St. Open Mon–Sat and Sun afternoon ♿. Phone 0131 225 7534)

⓱ WHISKY HERITAGE CENTRE

Here you'll find everything you ever wanted to know about Scotland's most famous product. (354 Castlehill. Open daily. Phone 0131 220 0441)

Glasgow

Tenement House: left, sitting room; right, kitchen

Mackintosh-inspired sign near the Willow Tearooms

Glasgow School of Art

Pollok House

When St Mungo built his tiny chapel on the banks of the Clyde 1400 years ago, he could scarcely have foreseen the vigorous, exciting and stylish city that stands there today. The name originally meant, in Celtic, the 'beloved green place', and to this day there are more parks here than almost any other British city.

Glasgow's proud of its history. Everywhere you go you'll see the city motto – 'Let Glasgow Flourish' – and its coat-of-arms. This commemorates the miracles of St Mungo. The fish (salmon, naturally) refers to the story of the queen of

Hunterian Art Gallery (AA)

Glasgow Cathedral

Cadzow (now the town of Hamilton, where Cadzow Castle still stands) who made the mistake of giving her wedding ring to a favourite courtier. The king, noticing its absence, stole the ring from the courtier and threw it into the river. Then, going to the queen, he demanded the ring's return on pain of death. In despair and penitence the queen went to St Mungo, who sent a man to the river to bring him the first fish he could catch. In due course the man returned with a fine salmon; the saint opened its mouth, and there was the missing ring. The tree on the coat-of-arms represents the frozen branch which St Mungo commanded to burst into flame in order to rekindle the holy fire at his monastery, and the bird is the robin belonging to a fellow saint, miraculously restored to life after being accidentally killed.

St Mungo's tomb lies in Glasgow Cathedral, recognized as one of the finest cathedrals in Europe. It is also one of the few sacred buildings in Scotland that survive from before the Reformation, which took place during the 1560s. These violent years, dominated by the great reforming

Winter Gardens, People's Palace (AA)

Royal Infirmary

Henry Moore sculpture outside the Burrell Museum

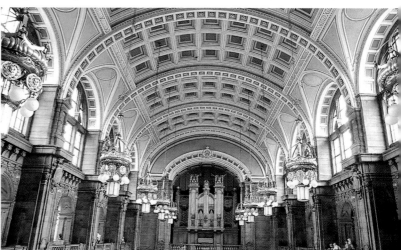

Ceiling detail,
Kelvingrove Art Gallery (AA)

Medieval stained glass, Burrell Collection (AA)

preacher John Knox, saw the destruction of churches and monasteries throughout Scotland as the people rose up against what was seen as the corruption of the Catholic Church. However the tradesmen's guilds of Glasgow stood firm against the mobs in defence of their beloved Cathedral, and though the statues were all destroyed the church itself survived.

It's hard to imagine now, but for centuries the Clyde was a relatively insignificant and shallow little river. Unlike other British trading cities Glasgow had to rely on a harbour 20 miles (32 km) away, at Greenock. After the union of England and Scotland in 1707 the city was able to

Green Bank Gardens, Newton Mearns, near Glasgow (AA)

trade freely with America. It was plain that fortunes were to be made in the tobacco industry. However, unless ships could bring their cargoes into the heart of Glasgow those fortunes would come no nearer than Greenock. Accordingly the ambitious project of deepening the Clyde was begun. After many false starts an engineer called John Golborne discovered, in 1771, that by narrowing the river the water could be made to flow faster and 'scour' out its own channel. He achieved this by building a series of dykes into the river. His work was continued later by the famous engineer Thomas Telford, who joined up the ends of Golborne's dykes to contain the Clyde within stone banks, rather like a canal. During the 19th century steam-powered dredgers took over the work of deepening the river. By the 1930s some of the world's largest vessels were being launched from Clydebank, and over 40 feet (12 m) of water flowed where people used to walk across the river at low tide.

It was the Clyde that brought Glasgow to the position of 'the second city of the Empire', and the greatest ship-building centre in the world. One of the most famous yards was that of John Brown & Co. at Clydebank. This was established in 1871

Princes Square

and proved an ideal site, being opposite the mouth of the River Cart. This meant that there was extra room to launch large vessels. In 1934 they needed every inch for the launch of the *Queen Mary*, over 1000 feet (300 m) long and drawing over 35 feet (10 m). Her sister-ship *Queen Elizabeth* and her famous successor the *QE2* also came from this yard. *The Lusitania*, whose sinking by submarine brought America into the First World War, was launched from here in 1906. The world's earliest steam ferry ran on the Clyde between Glasgow and Greenock. Most people can't believe how long

ago this started; the first service ran on 14 August 1812 (before the battle of Waterloo!). The ship (the *Comet*) was wrecked in 1820, but you can see a replica of her at Port Glasgow.

Things have changed on the Clyde. In the 1840s it was said that you could walk from one side of Glasgow Harbour to the other across the dense mass of shipping. Now the river is largely empty (but a lot cleaner). It's still important to Glasgow, though, and a trip down the river is a very pleasant way of passing an afternoon. It'll take you past the remaining working shipyards and out to the

St George's Tron Church (STB)

City Chambers (GTB)

City coat-of-arms

beautiful Firth of Clyde. This trip has been a favourite outing for Glaswegians for the last 150 years and there are many pleasant little resort towns along the coast.

It would be a mistake to see Glasgow as a city whose greatness is all in the past. It did go through a bad patch in the 1960s and 1970s with the decline of the ship-building industry, and the destruction, in some areas of the city, of its fine Victorian buildings, replaced by the standard concrete shoe-boxes of the time. But during the last ten years the city has undergone a renaissance

of confidence, and is a real pleasure to explore. Buildings have been cleaned, streets pedestrianized, and there is a great deal of really good new architecture which complements the handsome Victorian commercial buildings of the city centre. It's very much a young and fashionable city, with a colourful bar and café life. For a number of years it's also been the home of some of the best young British artists. Pay a visit to some of Glasgow's many commercial galleries (try the Compass Gallery, 178 West Regent Street) and see if you can spot the stars of the future.

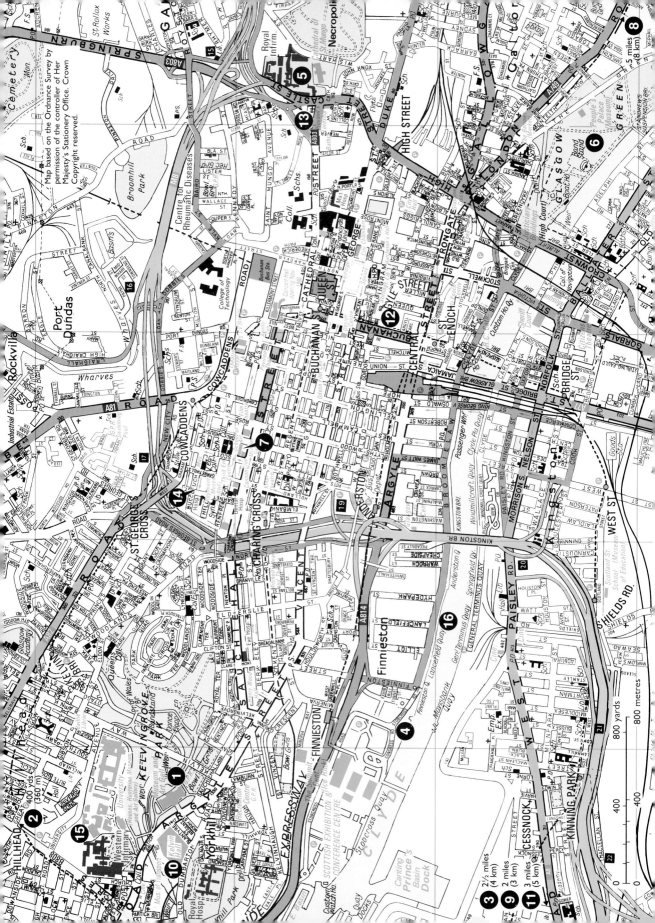

❶ ART GALLERY AND MUSEUM

One of the finest civic collections in Britain. Paintings include works by Rembrandt, van Gogh, Botticelli, Raphael, Picasso and the Scottish Colourists. Children (and adults) will enjoy the animal exhibits, armour and many other artefacts. Refreshments. (Kelvingrove. Open Mon–Sat and Sun afternoon ♿ ☕. Phone 0141 221 9600)

❷ BOTANIC GARDENS

Over 40 acres of woodland and open lawns in the heart of the city, with the River Kelvin running through. Here you'll find the remarkable Kibble Palace, a great Victorian greenhouse in cast-iron where white marble statues lurk among the tropical ferns. (Open daily ♿. Phone 0141 334 2422)

❸ BURRELL COLLECTION

One of the most extensive collections of foreign antiquities and other artefacts in the country, given to the city in 1944 by the ship-builder Sir William Burrell. The airy, modern gallery, a work of art in itself, stands in Pollok Country Park. The collection has over 8000 items, so it's nice to know that there is a very good restaurant for when your feet grow tired. (Open daily ♿. Phone 0141 649 7151)

❹ FINNIESTON CRANE

The largest dockside crane ever erected in Glasgow. It was built in 1932 and can lift 175 tonnes. It's powered by electricity and is still in regular use. Close by is the North Rotunda, a domed building housing a restaurant and bar.

❺ GLASGOW CATHEDRAL & ST MUNGO MUSEUM OF RELIGIOUS LIFE AND ART

Glasgow Cathedral was erected on the site of an earlier building between about 1240 and 1480. The crypt, some of which survives from the older cathedral, is probably the finest part, with magnificent fan-vaulting. The cathedral's treasure and archives were taken to France just before the Reformation, and never seen again. In front of the cathedral is Glasgow's new museum of religion, the first in the world to examine all the major religions. (Open Mon–Sat and Sun afternoon ♿. Phone 0141 553 2557)

❻ GLASGOW GREEN AND PEOPLE'S PALACE

The very first public park in Britain, opened in 1662. Nearby is the People's Palace Museum which tells the story of the city from 1175 to the present day, emphasising the lives of the people as well as events. Refreshments available. (Open Mon–Sat and Sun afternoon ♿. Phone 0141 554 0223)

❼ GLASGOW SCHOOL OF ART

Designed in 1896 by the pioneering architect Charles Rennie Mackintosh. An astonishing building, many years ahead of its time. The interior is just as remarkable, and there are usually good exhibitions. (167 Renfrew St. Open Mon–Fri. Phone 0141 353 4500)

❽ GLASGOW ZOO PARK

A splendid conservation zoo, set in beautiful parkland, and specializing in big cats and reptiles. Guided tours, picnic areas, children's attractions. Refreshments available. (Uddingston. Open daily ♿. Phone 0141 771 1185)

❾ HAGGS CASTLE

A 16th-century castle now run as a museum of history for young people. There are hands-on displays in period rooms, exhibitions and a changing programme of activities. (100 St Andrew's Drive. Open Mon–Sat and Sun afternoons. Phone 0141 427 2725)

❿ MUSEUM OF TRANSPORT

A wonderful collection of vintage cars, buses, trams, motorcycles, locomotives, fire engines and an imaginary Glasgow street of 1938. Refreshments. (Kelvin Hall. Open Mon–Sat and Sun afternoon ♿ ☕. Phone 0141 221 9600)

⓫ POLLOK HOUSE

Built around 1750 and given to the city in 1966 together with more than 360 acres of parkland, this forms the core of the Pollok Country Park. Quite apart from its fine 18th-century furnishings, it contains an excellent collection of Spanish paintings. Refreshments available. (2060 Pollokshaws Rd. Open Mon–Sat and Sun afternoon. Phone 0141 632 0274)

⓬ PRINCES SQUARE

A spectacular conversion of Georgian buildings into an enclosed centre just off Buchanan Street, filled with shops, cafés and restaurants on several levels, all linked by glass lifts and escalators.

⓭ PROVAND'S LORDSHIP

This is the oldest house in Glasgow, built in 1471 and now a museum with period displays. (3 Castle Street. Open Mon–Sat and Sun afternoons ♿. Phone 0141 552 8819)

⓮ THE TENEMENT HOUSE

A fascinating Victorian flat which has survived virtually unchanged since 1892. Contains furniture and domestic items of the family who lived here for more than 50 years. (145 Buccleuch Street. Open Mar–Oct daily, afternoons only. Phone 0141 333 0183)

⓯ UNIVERSITY OF GLASGOW

The University of Glasgow is a splendid example of the Gothic Revival style. Tours of the campus start from the Visitor Centre (phone 0141 330 5511). See also the Hunterian Museum with its world-famous coin collection, ethnographic and geological items (phone 0141 330 4221). The Hunterian Art Gallery has a major collection of works by Whistler and a replica of Charles Rennie Mackintosh's town house (phone 0141 330 5431). (University Avenue. All open Mon–Fri and Sat mornings)

⓰ *THE WAVERLEY*

If you'd like to make the trip down the Clyde, what better way than on the world's last sea-going paddle steamer? *The Waverley* now offers a regular service from the city throughout the summer. On board there's a restaurant and live entertainment at weekends. Anderston Quay. Phone 0141 221 8152.

Tayside and the East Neuk

Preceding page: **Landscape near Glamis**

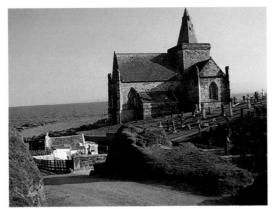

St Monans

Blair Castle, Blair Atholl (AA)

St Andrews

Stirling Castle

This area covers a great variety of landscape, from the rolling farmlands of Fife to the beginnings of real Highland scenery on the edge of the Grampians. For centuries this was the real heart of Scotland, and you'll find many of the most famous palaces and castles in this region.

Once you're past Perth you're beginning to get into the Highlands proper. The name doesn't really relate to the mountainous landscape (some parts are flatter than the Lowlands). It's more accurate to think of it as the territory of the Celts,

Rumbling Bridge, near Dollar

Crail

the Gaelic speakers. Scotland has always been ruled by English-speaking Lowlanders, while her fighting men have come from the Highlands.

Stirling and Arbroath are among the most important places in Scottish history. It was at Stirling Bridge that Sir William Wallace defeated an English army in 1297, and effectively cleared the English out of Scotland. This first attempt at independence was short-lived. The following year Edward I, the 'Hammer of the Scots', came himself to deal with the uprising and defeated Wallace at

53

Culross

From the Queen's View

Dalnaglar Castle, Glenshee

the battle of Falkirk. But the ground was now ready for the great Robert the Bruce, and it was he who fought Stirling's other great battle. This was Bannockburn, where on Midsummer's Day, 1314, the Bruce finally won Scotland's independence. His 5000 spearmen completely destroyed Edward II's army of 20,000, including thousands of cavalry, by driving them into the waters of the Forth and the Bannock Burn. A few years later the nobles of Scotland gathered at Arbroath Abbey where, in the Declaration of Arbroath, Scotland's independence was formally announced to the rest of the world.

Once you're across the Firth of Forth don't make the mistake of driving blindly north. If you do, you'll miss some of the prettiest fishing villages to be seen between here and Land's End. They're all on the coast of the East Neuk, the corner of Fife that sticks out into the North Sea. There's a chain of them along the coast, each more fascinating than the last. For centuries they traded with the Continent, which left its mark on the style of

Loch Achray, the Trossachs

The East Neuk coastline

building (the 'crow-step' gables, common in Belgium). Later on herring fishing became the main industry. This has declined recently, but is still important and each village maintains a small fleet. These are working villages still, not tourist centres. Lower Largo, with its fine sandy beaches, was the birthplace of Alexander Selkirk, the real Robinson Crusoe. Anstruther (pronounced Anster), the biggest port, is the home of the excellent Scottish Fisheries Museum. You can also go aboard the North Carr Lightship, moored in the harbour. One of Anstruther's more curious sights is the Buckie House. Buckie is the dialect word for shell, particularly for the tiny cowries that are found in a few places along the east coast. In the last century this house was lived in by a local eccentric whose ambition was to be buried in a shell-covered coffin. He collected so many that he was able to decorate his home with them, inside and out.

If it happens to be wet one day, make the most of your time and head for the town. Perth was the

Pittenweem

The Pineapple, Dunmore

Castle Campbell, Dollar

Scone Palace, near Perth

Pittenweem

ancient capital of Scotland and is filled with relics of its historic past. On a more modern note, children will love its indoor leisure pool. The other major city in the area is Dundee. This great port is reached by the Tay Road Bridge, built in 1966. It was the nearby Tay Rail Bridge which collapsed in 1879, with the tragic loss of 100 lives. Dundee was also the home of William McGonagall, infamous as the world's worst poet! While there, pay a visit to the recently opened Discovery Point at the quayside to see Captain Scott's research ship, *Discovery*. There are many smaller towns worth visiting, not

Falkland Palace

least historic Dunfermline and Arbroath. Don't miss Pitlochry, where you can see salmon leaping in the waters below the hydroelectric dam. Near here, incidentally, is the beautiful Queen's View over Loch Tummel, one of several in Scotland, named after Victoria. This one predates her, though, and may even be named after Mary Queen of Scots. She had many links with this area – in fact, she was crowned in Stirling Castle when only five days old. Loch Leven Castle was the scene of her imprisonment in 1567. She made a dramatic escape the next year, helped by her jailer's son who got her into a boat and locked the guards in the castle, throwing the keys into the loch. It's not just a romantic legend, as was proved when the bunch of keys was accidentally discovered in the loch 300 years later! The castle on its island can still be visited in summer.

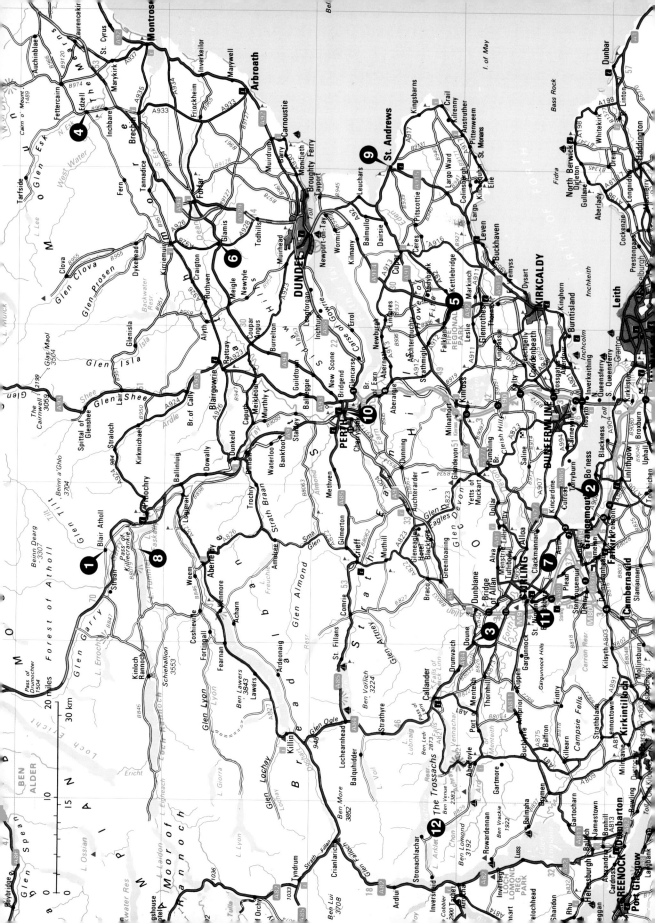

❶ BLAIR CASTLE

The home of the Dukes of Atholl. There's been a fortress here since at least 1269. What you see now isn't quite as old as it looks, though. After the Jacobite defeat in 1745 it became fashionable to imitate English style, so all the fortifications were removed to make a simple Georgian country house. Later on, of course, it became fashionable to be Scottish again, so all the gables, parapets and turrets were replaced during the 19th century. The family collection is wide-ranging and includes armour, porcelain, paintings, costumes, tapestries and toys. Refreshments are available. (Open Apr–Oct daily ⅋ ⅋. Phone 01796 481207)

❷ CULROSS

Given the status of Royal Burgh in 1588 due to its burgeoning trade with the Low Countries, this fascinating village (pronounced 'Cooross') has been painstakingly preserved by the National Trust for Scotland. Visit the Flemish-style Town House museum and early 17th-century Palace. (Open Easter–Oct daily. Phone 01383 880359)

❸ DOUNE

If you're interested in cars don't miss Doune Motor Museum, with Scotland's best collection of classic and vintage cars. (Open Apr–Oct daily. Phone 01786 841203) In April, June and September there are Hill Climb events. There's also a very well-preserved 14th-century castle in the town.

❹ EDZELL CASTLE

Once the most splendid castle in the area, it's now famous for its walled garden (1604). The walls are covered in unique symbolic panels with the family arms (Lindsay). Former flower-beds in the centre are surrounded by box hedges clipped into the family motto 'Dum Spiro Spero' – While I breathe I hope. (Open Mon–Sat and Sun afternoon. Phone 0131 244 3101)

❺ FALKLAND PALACE

This 16th-century palace has one of the best gardens in Scotland – the interior and contents are also worth seeing. Don't be surprised if the early Renaissance façades make you think of French châteaux: French stonemasons were used by James V to make his future bride (daughter of the French king) feel at home. (Open Apr–Oct, Mon–Sat and Sun afternoons ⅋. Phone 01337 857397)

❻ GLAMIS CASTLE

This huge castle, remodelled in the 17th century, has been the home of the Queen Mother's family since 1372. Princess Margaret was born here in 1930. Don't miss the world's largest sundial, 21 feet (6 m) high with 84 dials. The castle also has an attractive garden and nature trail. Refreshments are available. (Open Easter–mid Oct daily ⅋. Phone 01307 840242)

❼ THE PINEAPPLE

This extraordinary building in the shape of a giant stone pineapple has been restored by the National Trust. If you like, you can live in it – the Landmark Trust lets it out for holidays throughout the year. It was built in 1761 when pineapples were a fashionable rarity. (Open grounds, daily, 0930–sunset)

❽ THE QUEEN'S VIEW

A magnificent view (situated on the B8019) to the conical peak of Schiehallion, and the moor of Rannoch and mountains of Glen Coe beyond. Forest walks and visitor centre. (Open Apr–Oct daily)

❾ ST ANDREWS

This attractive town is most famous as the home of the Royal and Ancient Golf Club, founded in 1754 and now the game's ruling body. There's now a British Golf Museum which is of interest even to non-golfers. But St Andrews isn't just golf. The 12th-century cathedral, 13th-century castle and famous university should also be seen. Children will enjoy the Sea-Life Centre and there are festivals and fairs all year, including the medieval Lammas Fair in August. ☎ 01334 472021

❿ SCONE PALACE

This is famous as the crowning-place of the kings of Scotland from 843 until 1296. The coronations were performed upon the Stone of Scone (pronounced 'Scoon'), which originally came from Iona. In 1296 Edward I stole the Stone and took it to Westminster Abbey, where it still is – or is it? In 1951 a group of patriotic Scots secretly removed the Stone from Westminster and placed it in Arbroath Abbey (scene of the Scottish Declaration of Independence in 1320). In due course the police arrived to take it back again. However, many people believe that a copy was hastily made by a local stonemason, and it's the copy that sits under the Coronation Chair at Westminster. The present palace, built in 1803, has a fine collection of objets d'art. Adventure playground. Refreshments are available. (Open Easter–mid Oct, Mon–Sat and Sun afternoon; July–Aug, all day Sun ⅋ ⅋. Phone 01738 552300)

⓫ STIRLING CASTLE AND BANNOCKBURN HERITAGE CENTRE

Like Edinburgh Castle, Stirling stands on a spectacular outcrop of rock. The Old Town, with its cobbled streets winding steeply up to the castle, is not to be missed. The area is famous as the scene of the two greatest victories over the English. The first of these was the battle of Stirling Bridge. It is commemorated by the spectacular Wallace Monument nearby, where Wallace's great sword is preserved. There are vivid audio-visual displays, and a marvellous view from the top. The other was Bannockburn. You can follow the course of these events through the excellent exhibitions run by the National Trust on the site of the battlefield, where there is a huge statue of the victorious Robert the Bruce himself. (Phone 01786 812664)

⓬ THE TROSSACHS

A beautiful area of hills, lochs and forests, mostly within the Queen Elizabeth Forest Park. It is ideal walking country, and there are several lovely forest drives as well. You can find out about these at the Queen Elizabeth Forest Park Visitor Centre near Aberfoyle.

Marischal College, part of Aberdeen University

Shipbuilding, Aberdeen

Invercauld Bridge, River Dee

Preceding page: **Pitmedden Garden, near Oldmeldrum**

If you've chosen to come up the eastern side of Scotland, it's at Deeside that you begin to enter true Highland country. This area stretches from the Grampian Mountains to the lowland country around Aberdeen with its often spectacular coastline.

The River Dee is famous for its royal associations, for it was at Balmoral in the Dee valley that Queen Victoria and her husband chose to make their refuge from the court. Every monarch since then has followed suit, though none so enthusiastically as the present Queen. Victoria settled on Balmoral after a wet holiday in the western Highlands. Her doctor had suggested she try the drier eastern climate, and in 1848 she and Albert arrived in Aberdeen and travelled up the Dee valley. They both fell in love with Balmoral's situation, and Albert started negotiating to buy the estate. This took some time, but by 1852 Balmoral and a neighbouring estate belonged to the royal couple. Unlike other royal properties, it is still bequeathed as private property from monarch to monarch. By 1855 the new castle was ready for occupation. It must have been an amazing sight in

Falconer, Ballater

Field of rape near Balmoral

Victoria's day, with carpets, furniture and curtains all in Stuart tartan, while the walls were covered in a 'Scotch thistle' pattern. Perhaps this vivid colour-scheme helped to make up for the notorious Balmoral chill. Balmoral is now well hidden behind carefully planted woodland, but for a distant view of it take the A939 up towards Strathdon. If you follow the road along the Dee, look out for the charming white suspension bridges over it.

It was largely as a result of Victoria's real passion for the Highlands that the cult of 'Scottishness' spread throughout Britain. After the defeat of the Highlanders at Culloden in 1746, everything associated with the Highland way of life was banned – mainly dress, weapons and music. This lasted for 36 years until 1782, the year in which the Clearances began. It's worth noting that it was precisely as they were betraying their people during these cruel years that the Highland lords began to romanticize their own past. Sir Walter Scott played a great role in all this, and for the very good reason of wanting to give the Scots a sense of pride in their history. It was he who 63

Elgin Cathedral

Elgin

Crathie Church, Balmoral

persuaded George IV to visit Edinburgh, and not only that but to be seen wearing 'Highland dress'. The enormous pageant that Scott organized showed Highlanders as the colourful and gallant figures of his novels. (The few Highlanders sent from Sutherland were so ragged and wretched that they were not allowed in the procession.)

This was when the myth of the tartan was invented – there is no evidence whatever that it was used as a clan's identifying mark before about 1800. Imagine trying to distinguish those elaborate patterns in the smoke and dust of battle! It was during the 18th century that the kilt was invented – by an Englishman. He was an iron worker who noticed that his Highland employees either found the traditional long plaid too cumbersome to work in, or appeared practically naked when they took it off. The costume as we know it has evolved since

River Earn, Mill of Ross (EPL)

then, though the wearing of it had at first to be encouraged. In 1832 the Duke of Leeds put everyone on his Scottish estates into Highland dress, and Victoria did the same a few years later. Still, however dubious its origins, it does now have a longish history – and it's certainly one of the most glamorous costumes a man can wear at this end of the 20th century!

The lovely remains of Elgin Cathedral are not to be missed – actually, it's remarkable that there's anything to be seen at all. One hundred and fifty years after it was built it was burned down by the 'Wolf of Badenoch'. This savage man had been excommunicated by the Bishop of Elgin for his earlier crimes, and this was his revenge. In the 16th century the tower collapsed. Fifty years later the government stripped all the lead off the roof in order to pay its troops (the ship carrying the lead

Dunnottar Castle, near Stonehaven

Crathes Castle, Banchory

Strath Avon

away sank before it could be sold). The following century Cromwell's army smashed whatever they found still intact, and in 1711 the tower fell down again. A hundred years after that a poor shoemaker was given the job of looking after the ruins. It's entirely owing to his devoted labours that the cathedral is worth visiting today. His gravestone tells the story.

This area has many associations with Macbeth. He was the last Scottish king to rule as a Highlander and (in spite of Shakespeare) a just ruler by the standards of those times. He was killed by Malcolm not at Dunsinane but at

St Machars Cathedral, Aberdeen (AA)

Lumphanan, near Craigievar, in 1057. Forres, near Elgin, has been linked with witchcraft for centuries, and the 'blasted heath' where the witches met Macbeth is just outside the town. Whatever the origin of this tale, it's certain that three witches were put to death for casting spells on King Duncan. They were rolled downhill in spiked barrels before being burned – there's a stone commemorating the event outside the town. If you see it, have a look also at Sueno's Stone not far away. It's a mystery to archaeologists, over 20 feet (6 m) high and decorated with carvings of chariots, decapitated bodies and captives. The curious thing is that there is no historical record of the battle which it obviously describes.

This region is famous for its castles. The 16th-century examples of Brodie and Ballindalloch are particularly fine, exemplifying the transition from the defensive tower houses of the early 16th century to the country houses of the Victorian period. But Craigievar is the most beautiful of all. Don't be misled by its delicate appearance though; you'd be as safe here as anywhere.

Avenue at Craigievar Castle

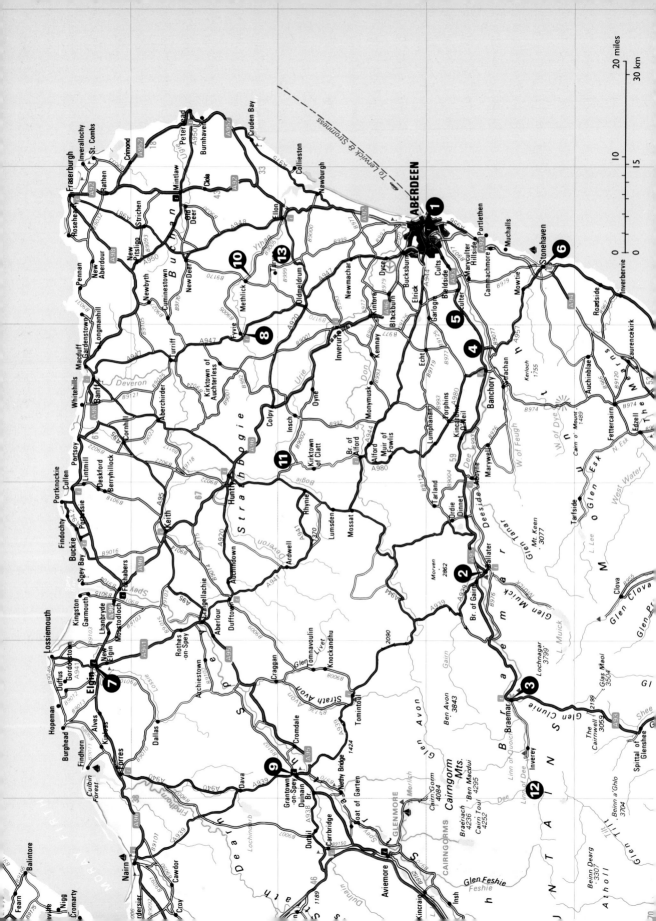

❶ ABERDEEN

Known as the 'Granite City', Aberdeen is the third-largest city in Scotland. It is a great fishing port and the oil capital of Europe. Don't be fooled by all this, though, because it's also a wonderful place to spend part of your holiday. It's an old city, and in and around the High Street you can visit the 500-year-old university and King's College Visitor Centre. You can't miss Union Street, the main shopping area – it's a mile long and 70 feet (21 m) wide. The fishing harbour is enormous and well worth exploring – take a look at the Maritime Museum afterwards. The city Art Gallery has a very fine collection. Don't miss Duthie Park and Winter Gardens, an award-winning modern park with masses to see. There are miles of sandy beaches and children of all ages will also enjoy the Satrosphere, where they can conduct their own scientific experiments. ☎ 01224 632727

❷ BALLATER

The railway station of this pretty spa town was originally the station from which Queen Victoria would alight when travelling to Balmoral. Pananich Lodge, the original spa, was founded in 1785 and was so successful that the facilities were expanded and the town of Ballater soon became fully established. ☎ 01339 755306

❸ BRAEMAR

This town is famous for the 'Gathering' held every September, attended by the royal family. This is the largest Highland Games in Scotland, dating from 1832. Here you can see the Tossing of the famous Braemar Caber, nearly 20 feet (6 m) long and weighing 132 lb. The history of the Gathering, as well as the town's royal connections, are shown in Braemar's Highland Heritage Centre. The 17th-century castle is unusual in that the curtain wall was built in the shape of a star. Don't miss the inscriptions inside, carved by lonely English soldiers in the 18th century, and the grim pit prison. ☎ 01339 741600

❹ CRATHES CASTLE

Pronounced 'Crathess', the castle dates back to the 16th century and is also well known for its 18th-century garden. The painted bedroom ceilings with their accompanying rhymes and proverbs are delightful. The huge yew hedges, clipped into elaborate topiary, were planted in 1702. Don't miss the enclosed Blue Garden. (Castle open Apr–Oct daily. Grounds open all year ♿ ❧. Phone 01330 844525)

❺ DRUM CASTLE

An impressive 13th-century tower-house, with later additions. It's run by the National Trust for Scotland, which has provided a playground and a 'wayfaring course' for children. (Open Easter–Sept daily; Oct, Sat and Sun afternoons. Grounds open all year ❧. Phone 01330 811204)

❻ DUNNOTTAR CASTLE

This castle's spectacular position makes it an experience not to be missed; sensible footwear advisable. St. Ninian founded a Christian enclave here in the 5th century, and Sir William Keith was excommunicated when he built the present castle in the 14th century on consecrated ground. During the Civil War the Roundheads besieged the castle in an attempt to win the Scottish Regalia. However, the local minister's wife was allowed through the English lines to visit another woman inside. When she left, it was with the Regalia safely concealed under her clothes. (Open Easter–Oct, Mon–Sat and Sun afternoon; winter, Mon–Fri. Phone 01569 762173)

❼ ELGIN

Standing on the banks of the River Lossie, this ancient city is famous for its glorious 13th-century cathedral, the 'Lanthorn of the North'. There is much to see in the area around the city: to the south, around the valley of the Spey, is the famous Malt Whisky Trail, featuring eight distilleries and a cooperage. ☎ 01343 542666

❽ FYVIE CASTLE

One of the finest habitable castles in Scotland, dating from the 13th century. Successive generations of owners have added to its grand structure. Its most famous feature is the 16th-century 'wheel' stair. There is also a very fine collection of portraits. (Open Apr, June, Sept, daily, afternoons only; July–Aug daily; Oct, weekend afternoons only ♿. Phone 01651 891266)

❾ GRANTOWN-ON-SPEY

This peaceful Georgian town was a favourite of Queen Victoria. The Spey is one of the great salmon rivers as well as also providing one of the basic ingredients for Scotland's best-known product, whisky. ☎ 01479 872773

❿ HADDO HOUSE

A very attractive Georgian house with terraced gardens built in 1731 by William Adam. Much of the interior is 19th-century Adam Revival. Refreshments available. (Open Easter–Sept daily; Oct, weekend afternoons only. Gardens and country park all year, daily ♿. Phone 01651 851440)

⓫ LEITH HALL

Unusual for this region, the hall is built round a central courtyard. It houses a very fine collection of militaria, which has been collected over many generations. Refreshments. (Open Easter–Sept daily, afternoons only. Grounds open all year ♿. Phone 01464 831216)

⓬ LINN OF DEE

A favourite spot of Queen Victoria's, where the Dee is channelled through a narrow cleft in the rocks. The bridge was opened by Victoria in 1857. Take care – more than one person has disappeared into the seething water.

⓭ PITMEDDEN GARDEN

The garden has been brilliantly restored to its original 1675 layout, with huge geometric flowerbeds marked out in box and yew, filled with combinations of colours. It is based on designs from Holyroodhouse. (Open Apr–Oct daily ♿. Phone 01651 842352)

69

West Central Highlands

Glen Coe

Preceding page: River Ba

Glen Orchy

The most lovely region in all the Highlands. The mountains of Glen Coe offer some of the most spectacular scenery in Scotland. To the west, the coast can be paradise on a still summer evening, when the sea shimmers like silk and the rocks are like black velvet against the sunset.

Here more than anywhere it's important to take your time if you're driving around. You'll have to in any case, because the roads seem to be narrower and more winding than anywhere else in Scotland. Allow plenty of time for your journey – especially if you're trying to catch a particular ferry – as it will take much longer than you might estimate

from looking at the map. Do take care on these single-track roads. Passing places are always marked with a white diamond. There's a universal etiquette that whoever's nearest to a passing place will stop (even if it's on the other side of the road) and let the oncoming driver through. Local people will assume that you know this rule! Also, if you're towing a caravan, or just enjoying the scenery, do let the driver behind overtake you – not everyone in Scotland is on holiday. Finally, never, never park in a passing place.

Great forests of oak and beech once covered much of this area. You won't see them now; the

The Black Mount, Clach Leathad

Abandoned croft

Duart Castle, Mull

last of them went to make room for the sheep, later the deer and now they have been replaced by conifers. But they had been largely destroyed even before the sheep arrived. During the 16th and 17th centuries wood was the cheapest fuel for the expanding iron industry. So much timber was needed for the iron furnaces that it was feared there would soon be no oak left for shipbuilding. For this reason the use of wood for smelting iron was banned in England, and coal-mining became more profitable. Wood was still cheaper, though, if you could get it, and so after the failed revolution of 1715, roads constructed under the 73

Glenfinnan Viaduct (EPL)

Fionnphort, Mull (EPL)

Ruined croft near Ardnamurchan

Oban harbour

Carving in the old abbey, Iona

command of General Wade made the huge untouched forests of the Highlands accessible for the first time. Although there were Scottish laws against the destruction of woodland, these could safely be ignored by the English. Iron foundries were soon set up all over Scotland and iron ore was shipped north in huge quantities. It was taken into the heart of the forests where temporary furnaces called 'bloomeries' were built. It was these furnaces that left the hills as bare and as barren as they are today. Near Taynuilt on Loch Etive you can see the remains of the last working bloomery in Scotland – it closed down in the 1870s when all the forests had gone. Incidentally you can also see the first monument to Lord Nelson here, erected by the English ironworkers as soon as the news of Trafalgar reached them.

In the shallower lochs and lochans (little lochs) you'll often see small circular islands fairly near the shore. These are called 'crannogs'. They are man-made islands, built 2000 years ago during the Iron Age, on which people would live in relative safety. Piles were driven into the bed of the loch, and brushwood and stone were then laid on top of them. Sometimes a causeway led to the crannog, but it would be barely wide enough for one person and was often laid in a zig-zag line to make it easier to defend against attackers.

As elsewhere in Scotland you'll see the shaggy forms of Highland cattle wandering the hills (and often the roads). They look friendly, but if you go too close when there are calves around you'll find out what those horns are for. They're incredibly tough little animals, spending even the harshest

Iona

Lochailort

Loch Eilt

winters out on the hills. Their thick coats protect them from any weather, and that matted fringe of hair keeps the driving snow out of their eyes. It is claimed that they foretell severe storms by performing the 'Dance of the Highland Cattle'. They are said to form a circle and then to take turns in order of age to leap and skip inside it. This is hardly ever seen, so don't be disappointed if they fail to perform for you!

If you're driving south towards Mull you'll pass through the beautiful scenery of Morvern and Kingairloch, south of Ardnamurchan. Beautiful but empty, because this was yet another area cleared by the infamous Patrick Sellar, the former land agent (or factor) for the Sutherland family. By this time he was no longer acting for the Sutherland family, but was a wealthy landowner in his own right. The men of Morvern formed associations to run communal farms, which were highly successful. But Sellar preferred empty land that he could use more profitably for sheep grazing than the rents his tenants could now pay him, and deliberately

Bonnie Prince Charlie, Glenfinnan

Peat

Loch Linnhe

targeted these communal farms for destruction. He wasn't the only landowner to do so. After the tenants had been evicted by the Gordons from the land around Loch Sunart, they took up residence on the barren little island of Oronsay. For the next 25 years they ran a successful communal farm there, until in 1868 the then Lady Gordon made them homeless again.

Iona is unique among the islands of the Inner Hebrides. Among so many beautiful, peaceful places it stands out for its atmosphere of utter tranquillity. As a community it owes its foundation to the tempestuous nature of its original founder St Columba. A powerful figure in his native Ireland, and founder of many monasteries there, he eventually quarrelled with the king, and fought and won a bloody battle with him. This led to his effective banishment from Ireland. With a dozen followers he settled on Iona in 563, and formed a community which by the time of his death in 597 was famous throughout Europe. No fewer than 60 kings lie in the graveyard around the abbey.

77

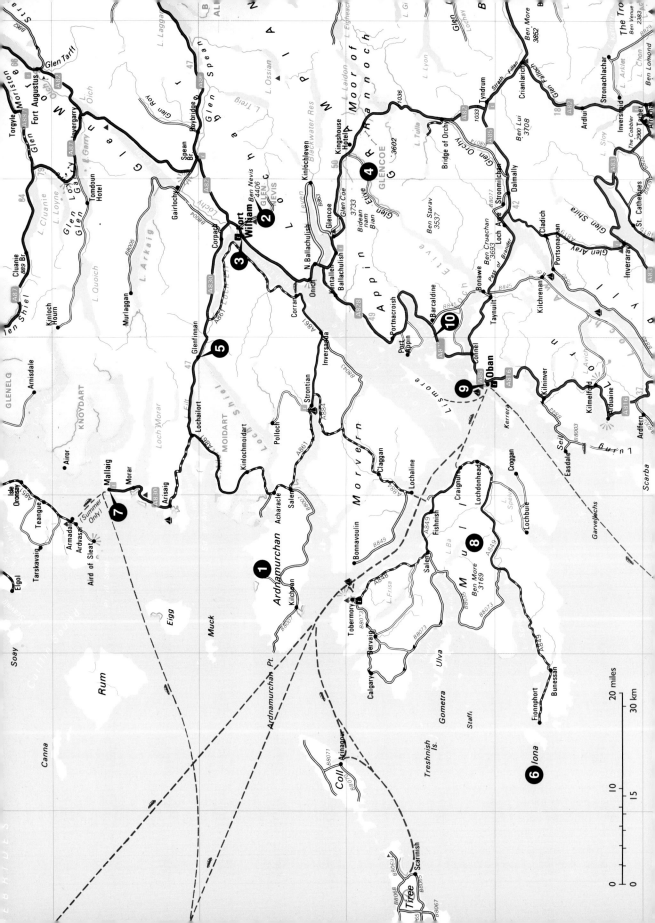

❶ ARDNAMURCHAN

This peninsula is the most westerly point of the mainland (20 miles/ 32 km west of Land's End). It is the most beautiful part of a breathtaking coastline. The wild landscape is volcanic in origin, and one of the results of this is that semiprecious stones can occasionally be found. Farther on there's the impressive 14th-century Mingary Castle overlooking the sea. On the northern coast there are the glorious white sand beaches of Sanna. You may be allowed to climb the lighthouse on the point. It's 114 feet (34 m) high, and the view from the top is quite simply out of this world.

❷ BEN NEVIS

The highest mountain in Britain, 4406 feet (1322 m) high. It is perfectly possible to climb it (allow a full day), but be ready for rapidly changing weather and go properly equipped. There are organized walks up the 'Ben'; for details contact Fort William tourist centre. There is a well-maintained footpath from Achintee Farm in Glen Nevis. Nearby, you can also hire mountain bikes or take a cable car to Aonach Mor, where there is a restaurant (phone 01397 705855).

❸ FORT WILLIAM

Fort William is the centre for tourism in the West Highlands. Here you should be able to find everything you need for a trip into the mountains. The town also has the excellent West Highland Museum. From Fort William you can take the train to Mallaig, a journey which takes you through a landscape of staggering beauty to the coast. ☎ 01397 703781

❹ GLEN COE

The most famous glen in Scotland, and the scene of the massacre of the Macdonalds in 1692. This treacherous act was carried out by the Campbells, so it is said, on the orders of William III. The Macdonalds had been five days late in taking their oath of allegiance to the King, at least in part through bureaucratic error. Campbell of Glenlyon and his troops had been living amicably with the Macdonalds for several days when they received their orders. The massacre began at dawn on 13 February with the slaughter of at least 40 men, women and children. The Signal Rock, near the Clachaig Inn (phone 01855 811252), marks the point where the murders began. This sombre glen is in the heart of some of the finest mountain scenery in Scotland, and you can view it from 2400 feet after a trip up the Glencoe chair lift, 12 miles south of Glencoe village off the A82. (Open Jan–Apr, June–Sept. Phone 01855 811303). Visit the Glen Coe Visitor Centre for information on walks in the area. Refreshments are available. (Open Apr–Oct daily. Phone 01855 811307)

❺ GLENFINNAN

This was the point, at the head of Loch Shiel, where Bonnie Prince Charlie started to rally the clans to his support in 1745. It's a very beautiful place, with the Prince's statue on a high column against a backdrop of mountains and water. The column was erected in 1815 by the grandson of one of the Prince's most loyal supporters, who died at Culloden. The monument is not to the Prince, but to the Highland dead; the statue was added in 1831. (Open all year daily) The National Trust for Scotland has a Visitor Centre here where you can follow the course of the campaign of 1745–46. Refreshments available. (Open Apr–Oct daily. Phone 01397 722250)

❻ IONA

This beautiful and tranquil island, home of the Iona Community, lies at the south-western corner of Mull. It's reached by ferry from Fionnphort (pronounced 'Finnafort'), or from Oban. Visitors are not allowed to take cars onto the island. ☎ (Oban) 01631 563122

❼ MALLAIG

The end of the West Highland Line, it is from here the ferries sail for the Hebrides. Until the railway arrived in 1901 this was one of the remotest communities in the Highlands, accessible only by 40 miles (64 km) of rough track or by sea. It rapidly became prosperous through fishing, though this has now declined with the advent of the factory ships. ☎ 01687 462170

❽ MULL

This is the largest of the Inner Hebrides. It's a lovely, peaceful island and not so rugged as Skye. It's reached by car ferry from Oban or Lochaline. Its centre is Tobermory, where a ship of the Spanish Armada lies wrecked in the bay. The surviving members of her crew were imprisoned in Duart Castle, at the eastern corner of the island. (Open May–Sept. Phone 016802 309) You can still see their cell in this 13th-century fortress, home of the Macleans since 1250. Not far away is the 19th century Torosay Castle, with pleasant formal gardens. Refreshments are available. (Castle open mid Apr–mid Oct daily. Gardens open all year. Phone 016802 421) There's a narrow-gauge steam railway to Torosay from Craignure (port for Oban). The world's smallest professional theatre, seating 38, is at Dervaig. ☎ (Tobermory) 01688 302182

❾ OBAN

This handsome and lively Victorian town is the main port for the islands. It is dominated by a miniature version of the Colosseum: this is McCaig's Tower, started (but never finished) in 1897 to relieve unemployment. You should visit Oban Distillery (Open Easter–Oct. Phone 01631 564242) and A World in Miniature (Open Apr–Oct. Phone 01631 566300), an unusual exhibition of tiny rooms, models and dioramas. North of Oban lie the ruins of Dunstaffnage Castle, overlooking Loch Etive from their precipitous outcrop, sandy Ganavan beach and the remains of 13th-century Dunollie Castle, once a MacDougall stronghold. ☎ 01631 563122

❿ SEA LIFE CENTRE

Located 10 miles (16 km) north of Oban, the Centre has over 30 fascinating displays, including Seal Pup and Fish Nurseries. (Open mid Feb–Nov daily; Dec–mid Feb weekends only ♿. Phone 01631 172386)

The Outer Hebrides

SCOTLAND

Preceding page: Lochfinsbay, Harris (EPL)

'Black house', South Uist

Hecla, South Uist (EPL)

Callanish, Lewis

Harvest, Enaclete, Lewis (EPL)

Croft, Barra (EPL)

Hebridean puffins (NTS)

Traigh Mhor airstrip, Barra (EPL)

82

The Outer Hebrides is a narrow string of islands, in most places rising no more than a few hundred feet, battered by the full force of the Atlantic. Sail west, and the first land you reach is the coast of Labrador. It sounds desolate. But you will find mile after mile of empty beaches with dazzling white sand, unbelievably clear water, and sunsets of tropical flamboyance.

The islands fall into two main groups. Lewis and Harris (actually one island) is the most northerly. If you listen to the shipping forecasts, one area will sound familiar. This is the 'Butt of Lewis', the most northerly point, marked by a lighthouse. The Lews, as it's called, is an area of about 60 miles by 20 miles (96 km by 32 km). The landscape tends to be flat and boggy, but the coastline makes up for this. Harris is steeper and rockier, one of the peaks rising to 2622 feet (785 m). Stornoway is the capital, and the biggest town in the Outer Hebrides.

North of Stornoway is the Black House at Arnol, a vivid re-creation of the old island way of life. There's also a very good local museum at Shawbost. Another sight not to be missed is the famous standing stones of Callanish. This great stone circle, with avenues radiating from it, is one of the best preserved sites in Europe. It is nearly 400 feet (120 m) from end to end. Nearby Dun Carloway should also be seen. This is a 'broch', or tower, dating from the Iron Age. These are unique to Scotland, and are the only known buildings of their age to have a double-skinned construction, rather like a cavity wall.

Below Lewis come the Uists and Benbecula – these are now connected by a causeway. Beyond South Uist lie the smaller islands of Barra and Eriskay. Gaelic is the first language of all these islands (except in Stornoway). It's many years, however, since the death of the last islander to speak no English at all.

Throughout the islands you'll find men and women hard at work weaving the Harris tweed. This famous cloth can be produced only in the Outer Hebrides. The Harris Tweed Association, formed in 1909, prevents imitations. It's a real cottage industry, most houses having a loom somewhere on which to work in odd moments.

It was from Rossinish on Benbecula that Bonnie Prince Charlie made his famous escape aided by Flora MacDonald. She had, at first, been unwilling to help him, but was eventually persuaded by his famous charm.

Eriskay has made the headlines twice in its long history. First as the spot where Bonnie Prince Charlie landed on his arrival from France in 1745. More recently, this is the island on which the *S.S. Politician* was wrecked with a cargo of 20,000 cases of whisky in 1941. This was the raw material for Sir Compton Mackenzie's hilarious novel *Whisky Galore*, and the wonderful Ealing comedy of the same name. Those bottles are now collector's items – not long ago one changed hands for several thousand pounds.

Barra is the southernmost of the larger Hebridean islands. It's a lovely, peaceful place. It has the only airfield in Britain that is under water twice a day – scheduled flights land on the beach at Eoligarry. Kisimul Castle stands on a small island in the bay. This was the home of the MacNeils, once a notorious family of pirates. They must have been magnificently vain as well – according to local legend, a servant was employed to stand on the battlements every day and announce "MacNeil has dined; Kings, Princes and the rest of the earth may now dine"!

It's important to remember that Sundays are treated with a degree of reverence on these islands that has long since disappeared in England. Do respect this point of view. The practical implications are that you are unlikely to find anything open, and you may find that some ferries will not run. Sunday observance is generally less rigorous on the Catholic islands such as Barra. (For information on all the sites mentioned, phone ☎ Stornoway 01851 703088)

The Central Highlands

Drinking fountain, Railway station

Duntulm Castle, Skye

Skye Croft Museum, Kilmuir

Clouttie Well, near Avoch

Preceding page: Loch Leathan, Skye

Flora MacDonald's grave, Kilmuir

Running right across Scotland, this region is rich in history and above all steeped in the dramatic history of Prince Charles Edward Stuart, the Young Pretender, affectionately known ever since as Bonnie Prince Charlie.

Charles Edward, grandson of James VII of Scotland and James II of England, was born and brought up in Rome after his father's three attempts to win the throne had failed. In 1745 he landed in Scotland, in the Western Isles, with promises of armed support from the French which never materialized. Despite this, on the 19th August 1745 he raised his standard at Glenfinnan. The chiefs were at first unwilling to support him,

Old Man of Storr, Skye

but they were gradually persuaded by Charles's courage and charm. A month later he marched into Edinburgh with his small force of about 1500 men. Here he held his famous ball at Holyrood, and the next day went on to Prestonpans, near Dunbar. On the 21st September he fought a ten-minute battle with General Cope, whose troops couldn't face the terrifying charge of the all-but naked and yelling Highlanders. After this his support increased among the chiefs, but only to about 8000 men. Many more either waited to see what would happen, or else remained loyal to the Government. The Highlanders marched into England, hoping for support from English Jacobites. Nearly all, however, could predict the failure of this attempted coup, and did not join the Highland forces. In December Charles' army reached Derby, and there was something of a panic in London. It's said that George II even had

Urquhart Castle, Loch Ness

Strathspey Railway (BR)

Corrieshalloch Gorge (AA)

nightmares about one of the most bloodthirsty chieftains, Glenbuchat, and would awaken crying in his German accent "Ze great Glenbogget is coming!"

By now, though, the English had rallied and new armies were being organized. Charles was persuaded to withdraw and make another attempt in the spring, and on 16 April 1746 he met the English army commanded by his cousin the Duke of Cumberland (son of George II) at Culloden. This bleak moor is the saddest and also the most important place in the Highlands, for it was here that Highland power was destroyed for ever. A tribal system that had lasted for centuries went with it. Cumberland was a young man, even younger than Charles, but he was also a trained soldier who had won great victories on the Continent. Events were to prove him a man of appalling cruelty as well. Even before the battle he was loathed in the Highlands. After he had stayed the night at Glamis Castle, the Jacobite household destroyed the bed he had slept in. In comparison,

Skiing in the Cairngorms (AA)

Sailing on Loch Morlich

after Charles stayed at Thunderton House in Elgin, his hostess kept his sheets for 25 years and was eventually buried in them.

The English army was equipped with artillery and made good use of it. The Jacobites had discarded their few cannon on the long retreat through England. Cumberland's guns played havoc with the Highland ranks long before they could charge. When they finally made the attempt, massed volleys of musketry prevented most of them from reaching the English lines. 1600 High- .

landers died in the battle for the loss of about 75 English troops.

Immediately after the battle Cumberland began to earn his title of 'Butcher'. Orders were given to kill every Highland survivor, starting with the wounded. The English army (at least a third of whom were Scots, more than a thousand being Highlanders) carried out the task with enthusiasm. Men were bayoneted and shot, and a number were burned alive. The destruction spread far and wide across Scotland, including the slaughter of the 89

Staffin Bay, Skye

Inverness

Loch Maree

Avoch harbour

wives and children of the Jacobite rebels, the looting and burning of their properties and the casual killing of many who had no connection with the rebellion. Clans loyal to the Government were given 'letters of fire and sword' to exterminate their hereditary enemies, and were well rewarded. The Duke of Argyll was paid £21,000 for his services (he had sent 1000 men to fight for the Government). The hunt was hardest for the Young Pretender himself. A loyal supporter who resembled the Prince claimed to be him, to delay the pursuers. He was immediately murdered. His head was taken to the Duke, who actually took it back with him to London. In England a flower was named after the Butcher. It was called Sweet William. In Scotland, they know the same flower as Stinking Billie!

The Prince eventually made his escape to France, living in hiding and protected by desperately poor men and women who ignored the £30,000 reward that was offered for his capture. There were high moments in this hunted existence – he held a three-day drinking contest on South Uist in the Outer Hebrides, and drank the rest of the party under the table. It was from here that he was rescued by the famous Flora MacDonald, who disguised him as her maid and brought him safely to Skye. This was the end of Stuart hopes. The Prince returned to Rome, took to drink, and died in 1788. He is buried in the crypt of St Peter's.

From Cairngorm across to Skye is wild and rugged country. For centuries it was almost impassable to anyone but Highlanders. It wasn't until the arrival of General Wade in 1724 that things began to change. He was initially sent to disarm the clans, but his far more successful work was in roadbuilding. The advantages of his labours were soon realized.

"Had you seen these roads before they were made, You would lift up your hands and bless General Wade".

He built no less than 40 bridges. Many chiefs disapproved of these, on the grounds that Highlanders might become soft!

There are plenty of waterfalls in Scotland, but few higher and probably none so spectacular as the Falls of Glomach. You reach these by road from Morvich, followed by a fairly rugged walk. The drop is just under 400 feet (120 m). Allow at least two hours there and back, and be careful on the footpath, especially when it's wet.

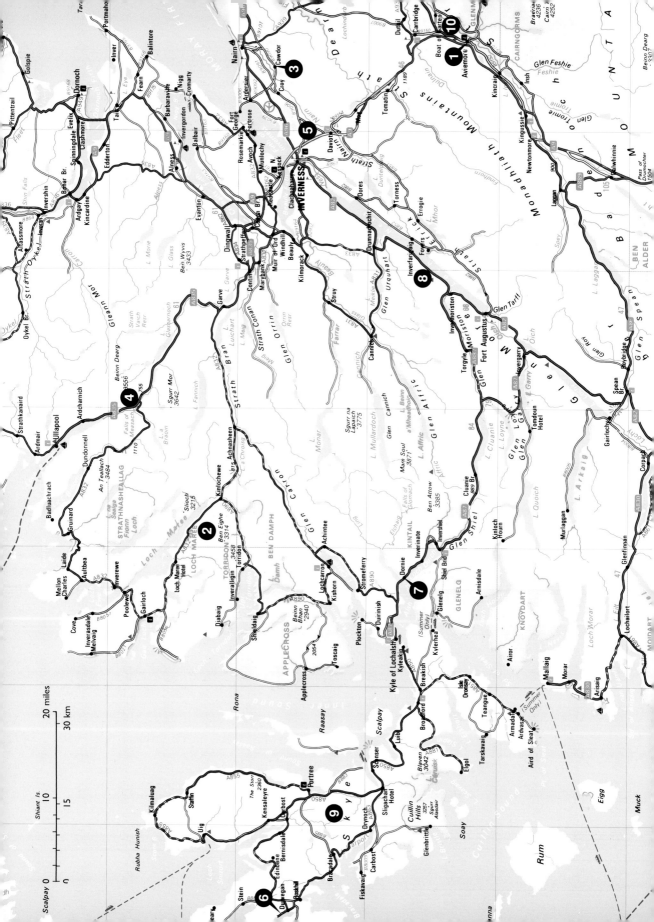

❶ AVIEMORE

Aviemore has become the holiday centre for the Highlands. Don't expect it to be picturesque – it was largely purpose-built in the 1960s – but it has every tourist facility you need, including a huge leisure centre for wet weather. It's famous as a skiing centre, and there's a dry ski slope for summer use too. Walking and climbing are the major activities in the area, and there's sailing on nearby Loch Morlich. ☎ 01479 810363

❷ BEINN EIGHE NATURE RESERVE

Created in 1951, this is Britain's longest established Nature Reserve. It's one of the last homes of the true wildcat. Other protected species include pine marten, golden eagle and badgers. (Open May–Sept, Mon–Sat. Phone 01445 760258)

❸ CAWDOR CASTLE

The castle, which features in Shakespeare's play *Macbeth*, was originally a 14th-century keep, before further fortifications were added in the 16th and 17th centuries. The gardens are beautiful and there are nature trails in the splendid grounds. There's also a mini-golf course and putting green which will keep the children amused. Refreshments available. (Open May–Sept daily ⛵. Phone 01667 404615)

❹ CORRIESHALLOCH GORGE

A really spectacular mile-long cleft in the rocks, with the 150 foot (45 m) high Measach Falls in the middle. You can cross them on a spray-soaked and swaying suspension bridge. Not for those with a fear of heights!

❺ CULLODEN

Culloden is the melancholy site of the last and perhaps the bloodiest battle ever fought on British ground, and where the Stuart ambitions for the throne vanished. The National Trust for Scotland runs a Visitor Centre here which explains the whole tragic tale. Refreshments available. (Open daily ⛵. Closed Jan. Phone 01463 790607)

❻ DUNVEGAN CASTLE (Skye)

This famous castle dating back to the 9th century is on the north-west coast of Skye. It's been the home of the MacLeods for at least 700 years. It's full of fascinating and bizarre relics, ranging from the 'Fairy Flag' (believed to have magical powers), to letters from Dr Johnson. There are also many items from Jacobite times, including a lock of Bonnie Prince Charlie's hair. Refreshments available. (Open mid Mar–Oct, Mon–Sat and Sun afternoon. Phone 01470 521206)

❼ EILEAN DONAN CASTLE

The castle's dramatic position on an islet in a tidal loch surrounded by steep mountains makes this one of the most photographed castles in the Highlands. Despite its historic appearance it's not as old as it looks. In 1719 the castle was garrisoned by Spanish troops supporting the Jacobite revolution. Three English men o' war sailed into the loch and completely destroyed the castle by cannon fire. The castle was rebuilt in 1932. (Open Easter–Sept daily. Phone 01599 555202)

❽ LOCH NESS

The loch is home (perhaps) of the world's best-loved monster. The loch is 24 miles (38 km) long, a mile wide and 900 feet (270 m) deep. You can find out more about the elusive monster at the Original Loch Ness Visitor Centre ⛵ (phone 01456 450342) and the Official Loch Ness Monster Exhibition ⛵ (phone 01456 450573), both at Drumnadrochit. There are also summer cruises with sonar equipment and even a submarine trip (phone 01285 760762). The loch is actually part of the Caledonian Canal. This runs the whole way across Scotland from Loch Linnhe to the Moray Firth. It was built by Thomas Telford from 1803 onwards, though it wasn't finished until 1847. At Banavie you'll find 'Neptune's Staircase', a 'ladder' of eight locks climbing 80 feet (24 m). The most famous landmark on the loch is the ruined Urquhart Castle. It was destroyed when it was blown up during the Revolution of 1689; the tower (16th century) is in good condition. (Open all year, Mon–Sat and Sun afternoon)

❾ SKYE

This beautiful island is the most easily reached of all the Inner Hebrides – just a five-minute ferry journey from Kyle of Lochalsh. Portree is the island's capital, sitting on the shores of a sheltered bay, which makes it pleasant for boating. Further afield are the monument to Flora MacDonald at Kilmuir, and the Clan Donald Centre in Armadale Castle, telling the story of Clan Donald and the Lords of the Isles. The Skye Croft Museum depicts island life in the 19th century. But above all, Skye is a paradise for climbers and serious walkers. The Cuillin peaks in particular are famous (in winter they offer harder climbing than the Alps). Even if you're not a walker but enjoy fine views, you will find beauty and diversity in every corner of this landscape: contrast the green and fertile southern peninsula of Sleat with the rugged, rocky spurs of Trotternish to the north, while in the west there are rolling hills and glorious sunsets with a backdrop of the MacLeods Table summits. Skye has had a chequered and often difficult history, and the monuments to past times can be seen in the many castles, brochs, standing stones and townships which have remained relatively untouched through the years. ☎ 01478 612137

❿ STRATHSPEY STEAM RAILWAY

Pride of the line No. 828 was built for the Caledonian Railway in 1899. This magnificent blue engine hauls trains on this mainly volunteer-run, full-scale steam railway between Aviemore (Speyside) station and the village of Boat of Garten. The railway has its own buffet car as well as a regular luncheon service. (Phone 01479 810725)

Red deer stag (NTS)

Dornoch Cathedral (STB)

Dunrobin Castle, Golspie　　　　**River Helmsdale** (STB)

Preceding page: **Loch Fleet**

Eas Coul Aulin waterfall (STB)

Sutherland is a region of thousands of square miles of the wildest and emptiest country in Britain, running from the storm-battered and unapproachable cliffs of the western coasts to the snug little fishing harbours on the east. Unbeatable for lonely beauty, either in spring with snow on the mountain tops, or in late summer when the hills are purple with heather and vanish into a distant heat-haze.

Empty these hills certainly are, and the reason for this desolation is well known. It was the region where the worst of the many injuries suffered by the Highlands over the centuries took place, known today as the Highland Clearances. The clan was a family – the word originally meant 'children' – and most of its members were at least distantly related by blood. As in most other tribal societies, land was owned by no-one and held in common for all. The chief was the 'father' of the clan, and was responsible for administering justice.

Ben More Assynt (TB)

In return he received not rent, because the land wasn't his to let, but the service of the young men as warriors. This changed over the years, and by the time of the second and last of the Jacobite rebellions, in 1745, the clansmen were paying minimal rents to their chiefs, but as men who looked after the clan, not as landlords. After Culloden everything changed. Besides the ban on Highland clothing and weapons the chiefs lost their rights of 'pit and gallows', the power of life and death which they had previously held over their people. They had become simply landlords, and now perceived their first duty to be to themselves. London was *the* place to be, and being fashionable cost a great deal of money.

The means for raising money soon appeared. It came in the form of a new breed of sheep, the

97

Ullapool, Loch Broom (AA)

Cape Wrath lighthouse (AA)

Faraid Head, Durness (STB)

Cheviot, which was hardy enough to withstand the Highland winters, and gave more and better quality meat and wool. The drawback was that they needed vast areas of the poor upland pasture in the summer, and would fill the narrow valleys when they were brought down for the winter. It was in these valleys that the clansmen lived, in small townships a mile or two apart. They were so well populated that the people were rarely out of sight of a settlement. But the rents they could afford to pay were small, and when times were hard the chief had a traditional obligation to care for them. But with their new-found positions in society to maintain the people were evicted to make way for the sheep. The people left passively and heartbroken, unable to understand why their once beloved chiefs and protectors were causing such hardship. They were sent either to the poor coastal lands, or shipped to North America.

The largest single landowner in the area was Lord Stafford, later the first Duke of Sutherland. He was English, and his wife had inherited the chieftainship of the people of Sutherland. It was in his name that the first large-scale evictions took

Dornoch Highland Gathering (STB)

Herding sheep (SCOTTISH TB)

place. For the first 20 years the Clearances were organized by his factor (Scottish land agent); a man named Patrick Sellar who conducted them with increasing brutality and ruthlessness, making his own fortune in the process. Many thousands went from the Sutherland estates alone between 1800 and 1841. The Clearances weren't an affair of distant history, but were to continue into the second half of the last century. As late as 1853 Mrs MacDonell, widow of the 16th Chief of Glengarry, supervised the burning of her people's cottages at Knoydart. A ship stood by to take them to America. Those who refused to go were left without shelter to die in the hills. Having cleared the estate she was then able to sell it at a better price. It wasn't until the 1880s that the Crofter's Acts were passed, providing security of tenure.

There's no doubt that change had to come. But the opportunity to create a widespread prosperity in the Highlands was thrown away in order to profit a few. Worse than all this, though, was the complete betrayal of the people by their chiefs. For them it was incomprehensible. Some felt that it was Divine retribution for some unknown sin.

Castle Ardvreck, Loch Assynt (WCA)

Suilven (WCA)

Inverewe Gardens, Poolewe

Perhaps the most moving of all the records of those days are the inscriptions scratched on a window of the church at Croick (15 miles/24 km west of Dornoch). Written by the Rosses of Glencalvie after their eviction, one of them reads 'Glencalvie people the wicked generation'.

The end of the 19th century saw the rise of the vast Australian sheep ranches, and as a result the slow fall in value of the Scottish sheep-runs. However there was a profitable substitute ready in the shape of the red deer. Huge areas of country-side were turned over to deer forest – open moorland, in fact, since both sheep and deer destroy woodland faster than anything else. Even in the 1970s there were nearly three million acres of deer forest. It's a success story for the deer, at least – in 1682 they were so rare that a law was passed banning the sale of venison. Nowadays

Lochinver (WCA)

they're carefully managed to keep the numbers constant, which involves culling about one-sixth of them each year.

After sheep and deer comes the third great money-spinning Highland activity – forestry. The Forestry Commission is actually Scotland's biggest landlord, owning about two million acres, of which about half are forest. Much of Scotland was once covered with pine and birch forest. Most of the forests have now disappeared as they were felled as fuel for iron furnaces, and increasing numbers of sheep and deer devoured the young seedling trees that would grow on to ensure the survival of the forests. Remnants of these forests remain, while elsewhere their place has been taken by sheep walks, deer and grouse moor and extensive conifer plantations. Only now are attempts being made to save these remnants by fencing out deer and sheep and by replanting new forests with seed from remaining old trees.

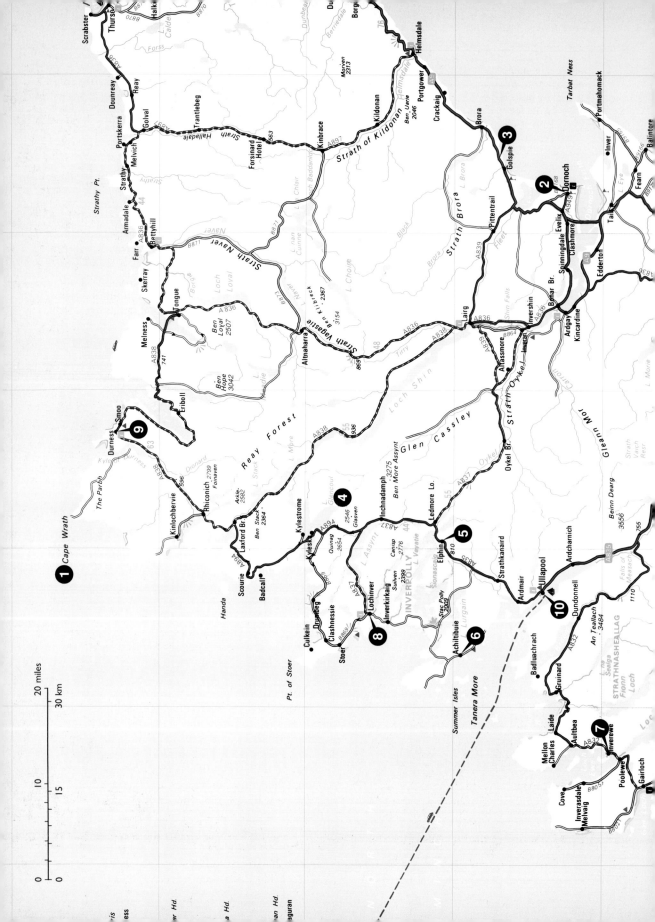

❶ CAPE WRATH

It's an appropriate name for this wild and lonely spot, with the sea beating against the base of the 400 foot (120 m) cliffs. In fact the name is a happy accident; it comes from the Norse word 'hvarf', meaning a turning place. As you'd expect it's an outstanding place for bird-watching, especially for gannets. The biggest colonies are to be found on the Clo Mor cliffs, which at 920 feet (276 m) are the highest on the mainland. It's an area primarily for walkers, as there is no access for cars. In summer there is a passenger ferry from Keoldale across the Kyle of Durness, which connects with a minibus service to the cape. The lighthouse was built in 1828. ☎ 01971 511259

❷ DORNOCH

A very attractive town dominated by the 13th-century tower of the cathedral. As well as miles of good beaches, the area surrounding the town is also famous for its golf courses. In 1722 it saw the last execution of a witch in Scotland. The poor woman was tarred, feathered and roasted alive. The former town jail is now a crafts centre where tartans are woven. ☎ 01862 810400

❸ DUNROBIN CASTLE

This vast 19th-century Scottish baronial style building is based on a 13th-century castle. It is the home of the Sutherland family, best remembered for their role in the Highland Clearances during the 19th century. The interior is worth visiting for its enormous and occasionally eccentric collection of family memorabilia. It gives a vivid picture of ducal life in the last century. Refreshments are available. (Open Easter, May–Oct, Mon–Sat and Sun afternoons. Gardens open all year. Phone 01408 633177) From the terrace there is a fine view over the formal gardens and down to the sea beyond. On nearby Ben Bhraggie you can't miss the enormous monument to the first Duke of Sutherland. It was erected in 1834 and stands over a hundred feet (30 m) tall.

❹ EAS A'CHAUL ALUINN

At 658 feet (198 m) this is the highest waterfall in Britain (three times as high as Niagara Falls!). It's perfectly possible to reach it on foot, though it'll take you half a day there and back. An easier way is to take a boat from the little harbour at Kylesku. The fall is at the far end of Loch Glencoul. There is a little inn at Kylesku that is well worth a visit; it's not every-where you can watch seals playing in the loch while you eat your breakfast.

❺ THE HIGHLANDS AND RARE BREEDS FARM, ELPHIN

Children will love this croft where they can meet many of the traditional breeds of Scottish farm animals, including the seaweed-eating Soay sheep. There's a feed round at 10 o'clock in the morning when they can help feed the animals. (Open mid May–Sept daily. Phone 01854 666204)

❻ THE HYDROPONICUM

This astonishing place can be found at Achiltibuie overlooking the lovely Summer Isles. Its creator, Robert Irvine, spent many years developing techniques for growing plants in water. Sounds impossible, but the proof of the success is here for all to see. At the Hydroponicum you can pick fresh strawberries every day between April and October, as well as bananas, passion fruit, lemons and all the ordinary garden vegetables and herbs. The space-age greenhouses provide three distinct and carefully-controlled climates – Hampshire, the Canaries and Bordeaux. Well worth the drive, and the Achiltibuie peninsula is exceptionally beautiful. Guided tours. (Open Easter–Sept. Phone 01854 622202)

❼ INVEREWE GARDEN

Many people think that this is the finest garden in Scotland, and one of the most remarkable in Britain. It is beautifully maintained by the National Trust for Scotland. The gardens were started in 1862 by Sir Osgood Mackenzie from 60 acres of bare and exposed hillside overlooking Loch Ewe and battered by salt gales off the Atlantic. His first step was to plant a windbreak of Scots pines. During the 20 or so years while these were growing he added vast quantities of topsoil and seaweed to the stony ground, all carried to the area in baskets. With soil and shelter established, the warm Gulf Stream climate made it possible to establish a sub-tropical garden in the latitude of Siberia. The rhododendrons are famous, but there is plenty to be seen here at all times of the year. Tree-ferns, giant forget-me-nots from the Pacific, some of the world's largest magnolias and climbing hydrangeas make this a gardener's delight. (Open all year daily ⑁. Phone 01445 781200)

❽ LOCHINVER

This village is a good holiday centre from which to explore the little roads that wind around the coast. It's on the edge of the Inverpolly Nature Reserve, and is dominated by the massive form of Suilven, the peak that many claim to be the most beautiful in Scotland. You can take wildlife and fishing cruises from here, and the energetic can hire mountain bikes to explore the glens. ☎ 01571 844330

❾ SMOO CAVE

This series of enormous limestone caves lies about 2 miles (3 km) east of Durness, the closest village to Cape Wrath and Scotland's most northwesterly village. The outer chamber is easily accessible and is the biggest at 200 feet (60 m) long and 120 feet (36 m) high. The next cave has an 80 foot (24 m) water-fall pouring into it, and is accessible only by boat (trips June–Sep). ☎ 01971 511259

❿ ULLAPOOL

This pretty Highland fishing town is the main port for the northern Hebrides. It was purpose-built as a fishing centre in 1788 by the British Fisheries Society to a plan by Thomas Telford. Large factory ships, many from Eastern Europe, can be seen anchored offshore in season. Ullapool is an ideal base for making trips by boat to the Summer Isles to see seals and birdlife. ☎ 01854 612135

Caithness and Orkney

Wicker chairmaking, Orkney (CT)

War memorial near Wick

Stromness (CT)

Stacks of Duncansby, Caithness

This is a region of flat, open moorland, rich in wildlife, with precipitous cliffs dropping to the sea. When you stand looking at the low hills of Orkney on the horizon, you're nearer to the Arctic Circle than you are to London. On clear summer days this can feel like the edge of the world.

If you want to make the most of every minute of your time here, arrange your holiday for the three weeks either side of Midsummer's Day. You're so far north that there's no true nightfall during this period, nothing more than a light twilight known as the 'simmer dim'. You'll find you hardly want to go to bed! If you're going on holiday with children, it's worth bearing in mind that in the northernmost areas of Scotland nearly all the activities are outdoor ones, and it's no good denying that it can sometimes be very wet and windy. Check the local forecasts regularly, or you may find yourself spending a lot of time in cafes with your bored offspring. The most reliable months for good weather are May and September, which are also relatively midge-free.

The most famous resident of Caithness is Her

Brodgar Stone Circle

Kirkwall, Orkney (CT)

Majesty the Queen Mother. Following the death of her husband in 1952 she bought the 16th-century Castle of Mey, between John O'Groats and Dunnet. The Royal Yacht *Britannia* brings members of her family to visit her each summer when she is in residence here, docking at Scrabster. Over the years she has created a magnificent garden. This is open to the public on three days a year during July and September. The dates change each year, so check with the local tourist office.

Orkney was first occupied by Pictish settlers about 2000 years ago. They were reached very

early by the missionaries, and by the time the Norsemen arrived the inhabitants were already largely Christian. A lot of island names begin with Papa, which is the old Norse name for a priest. Orkney became officially Norse when it was annexed in 875 by Harold Haarfagr, and for the next 400 years was governed by Norsemen taking the title of Earls of Orkney. It wasn't until 1468 that the islands were ceded to Scotland as part of a marriage settlement (in fact it's possible to argue that in law they still belong to Norway). The Norse influence has remained strong – even the

St Magnus Cathedral, Orkney (CT)

Italian Chapel, Lamb Holm, Orkney (CT)

Graveyard near Lybster, Caithness

Balblair distillery (GB)

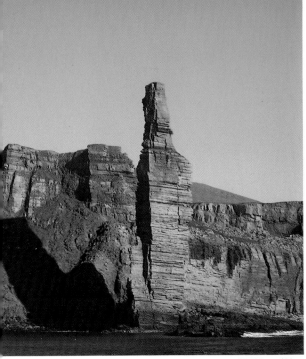

Old Man of Hoy

Fishing trawler off Lybster

local accent is more Scandinavian than anything else. The old Norse language – Norn – survived into the last century in Shetland. Place-names ending in '-by' or '-brough' are Norse in origin, while names beginning with 'pit-' may often be Pictish. You'll upset an Orcadian if you refer to him as Scottish. England and Scotland are equally foreign to the Orkneyman. If you hear someone say that they're going to the mainland they won't mean Scotland – the largest island of the Orkney group is called Mainland. Incidentally the group contains another 66 islands besides this one.

The great Pictish secret was said by the Romans to have been the art of making their heather ale, a

Skara Brae, Orkney (CT)

drink of magical potency. Sadly, the secret went with them. The last Pict to know the art is said to have hurled himself into the sea sooner than reveal it. The Picts may be the best-known of the old inhabitants of the country, but they certainly weren't the first. Like Orkney, Caithness is filled with relics dating back to the Stone Age, 5000 years ago. The Grey Cairns of Camster are from this period. They are impressively large stone tombs (which you can enter), the largest being 200 feet (60 m) long. Building it is thought to have meant moving about 3000 tonnes of stone. Rather younger is the Bronze Age 'Hill O'Many Stanes'. This consists of long rows of standing stones aligned roughly north-south. There's a theory that it formed a kind of calendar, as Stonehenge is said to have done.

At Marwick Head on Mainland you'll find a monument to Lord Kitchener, who died off this coast while sailing to Russia in 1916. The ship carrying him was lost with all hands when it was either mined or torpedoed.

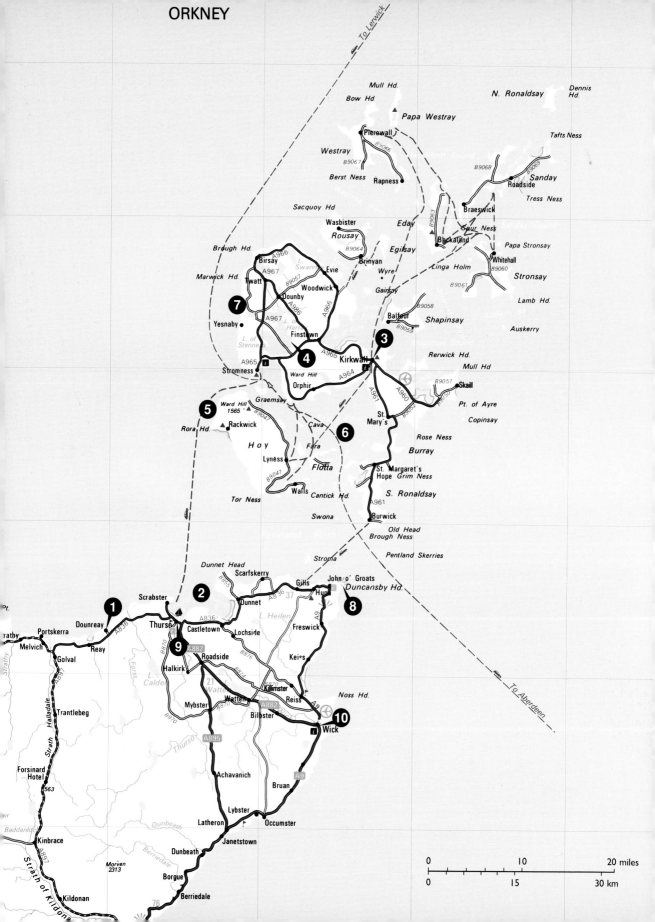

ORKNEY

❶ DOUNREAY

Visitor Centre and guided tours of this prototype fast-breeder reactor. (Open Easter–Sept daily. Phone 01847 802121)

❷ DUNNET BAY

A really magnificent white sand beach stretching for several miles. The village has a very pretty simple church with a tower which may date back to the 14th century. It's well worth making your way out to Dunnet Head, the most northerly point of the mainland (farther north than John O'Groats). There is a lighthouse on top of the 400-foot (120 m) cliffs, and the view of the island of Hoy, in Orkney, is superb. It's also a very good place to see colonies of puffins.

❸ KIRKWALL (Orkney)

This is the capital of Orkney (never 'the Orkneys'). It's famous for its great Cathedral of St Magnus, founded in 1127. It was built by Rognvald, nephew of the murdered St Magnus. When the Cathedral was restored at the beginning of this century, their bodies were discovered hidden inside the great central pillars in the choir. The body of St Magnus was identified by the wound in his skull. At the Reformation the building was saved from destruction by the people of Kirkwall. ☎ 01856 872856

❹ MAES HOWE (Orkney)

This vast Neolithic tomb is one of the finest in Europe. It's 25 feet (7 m) high and 115 feet (35 m) in diameter, built of huge stones weighing up to 3 tonnes. Look at the smoothness of the masonry, and then think that these people had only flints as tools – it's an astonishing piece of work. It was originally filled with treasure. However, in 1150 a group of Norsemen had to spend a winter here. They broke into the tomb and removed the treasure over three nights. The runic inscriptions they left recording all this can still be seen – one of them saying that the treasure was buried somewhere to the north-west of the tomb. If true, then it's still there. (Open Mon–Sat and Sun afternoons. Winter times vary. Phone 0131 244 3101)

❺ THE OLD MAN OF HOY (Orkney)

Many people will be familiar with this 450 foot (135 m) column of sandstone on the edge of the sea as a result of the televised climbs made a few years ago. It was first climbed in 1966, and the biggest hazards are apparently the attacks of furious seabirds – a bit of a distraction when you're 400 feet up and negotiating an overhang. It's normally visited by boat from Stromness. You'll also see the highest sheer cliff in Britain. This is St John's Head, rising 1140 feet (342 m) vertically from the sea breaking at its foot. ☎ (Stromness) 01856 850716

❻ SCAPA FLOW (Orkney)

A huge natural harbour almost 10 miles (16 km) across. This was a major naval base in the two world wars. In both wars a German submarine managed to enter the harbour and make successful attacks; on the second occasion, just five weeks after the outbreak of war, the Germans sank *HMS Royal Oak* with heavy loss of life. At the end of World War I most of the German fleet was ordered here after their surrender. Soon after their arrival nearly every vessel was sunk by its crew before they could be taken over. Don't miss the Italian Chapel on nearby Lamb Holm. This was built from scrap metal by Italian prisoners of war, and beautifully painted inside. It was restored by one of the original builders on his return to Scapa Flow in 1960.

❼ SKARA BRAE (Orkney)

This Stone Age village dating from about 2000 BC is fascinating for its glimpses of domestic life so many years ago. It's been preserved by being buried in sand (this may have originally destroyed the community). In 1850 a storm uncovered the site after a period of 4000 years. You can see beds and other primitive furnishings all made from local stone in the little group of single-roomed houses. There are even tanks in which the occupants are thought to have kept fresh fish or shellfish. (Open all year daily. Phone 0131 244 3101)

❽ STACKS OF DUNCANSBY

The stacks lie just south of Duncansby Head, the north-east tip of Scotland. You can walk to them from the car park. Take care, though – the grass grows to the very edge of these 200-foot (62 m) cliffs, and the winds can be strong. The nearest stack is called the Knee. When the tide is ebbing, the flow of water between it and the shore is so fast that the surface of the sea at this point actually slopes downwards. This well-known and dangerous phenomenon is locally called 'the Rispies'. The highest stack, Muckle Stack, is nearly 300 feet (90 m) high. Seabirds in vast numbers nest here. A good way to see them is from the sea; you can take a boat from John O' Groats. You should see puffins, guillemots, cormorants, kittiwakes, fulmars and many others. ☎ (John O' Groats) 01955 611373

❾ THURSO

The most northerly town on the mainland, Thurso derives its name from Thor, the Norse god of war. It actually means 'Thor's River'. You'll often see salmon leaping at the mouth of the river on their return from their annual migration to Greenland. The 18th century harbour is attractive. The town originally depended on the export of paving slabs or flagstones, before the days of concrete. These were exported all over Britain and even abroad. Ferries for Orkney sail from the nearby port of Scrabster. ☎ 01847 892371

❿ WICK

A hundred years ago this pleasant fishing town was Europe's largest herring port, with more than a thousand fishing boats to bring in the 'silver darlings', as the fish were known. As elsewhere in Scotland, this ended with the arrival of the huge factory ships in the 1960s which effectively cleared the seas of fish. The award-winning Wick Heritage Centre by the harbour tells the story of the town's great days (Open June–Sept, Mon–Sat). It contains everything from a full-scale harbour to a working lighthouse. ☎ 01995 602596

Page numbers in italics indicate a gazetteer entry